STILL GOING AGAINST THE GRAIN

WHEAT-FREE COOKERY

by

Phyllis Potts

Central Point Publishing
21861 S. Central Point Road
Oregon City, Oregon 97045
©1994 by Phyllis Potts

Printed in the United States of America
First Edition

Library of Congress Number 94-094308

ISBN 0-9630479-1-4

Potts, Phyllis L.
    Still going against the grain: wheat-free cookery/ Phyllis L.
Potts.—Oregon City, OR : P.L. Potts,

        p. ; cm.

    SUMMARY: Wheat-free recipes, most of which are also
grain and dairy-free,with an emphasis on breads and bread
machines.

    1. Wheat-free diet--recipes.   2. Food allergy--diet therapy-
recipes. I. Title.
RC588.D531 P   641.5'631 20

Cover design by Bruce DeRoos
Book design and page layout by DIMI PRESS

Every effort has been made to locate the copyright owners of
the material quoted in the text. Omissions brought to our
attention will be credited in subsequent printings. Grateful
acknowledgment is made to those publishers who asked that
their ownership be noted.

From the treasure box...

I wish to acknowledge...

Husband, Ed, for his tasting and his
        support.
Children, Natalie, Harvey and Neal for
        their encouragement.
Dick Lutz for his guidance and patience.
Emily Orlando, instructor, editor and friend.
Dr. John A. Green M.D. for his comments
        and suggestions.
Beyondesign, Seattle, for promotional
        graphics.
Ben Woodworth, Login Publishers
        Consortium, for always having time.
Marilyn, Chris & Jonette of Dr. Craig Smith's
        office in Oregon City.
Bob's Red Mill for their contributions to the
        effort.
Mary Lutz for strawberries and input!
My co-workers at Clackamas Community
        College Library for their support.
To all who tasted and said, "Put it in the
        book!"

If I can stop one Heart from breaking
I shall not live in vain.
If I can ease one Life the Aching
Or cool one Pain

Or help one fainting Robin
Unto his Nest again
I shall not live in Vain.

Emily Dickinson

FOREWORD

In 20 years of medical practice, I've found that the most powerful influences on health and disease are nutrition and the patient's attitudes and beliefs. We can change our diet and observe the effects. Our belief system cannot be changed directly, but the commitment to eat healthy, non-allergic food frequently helps to heal harmful attitudes and self-limiting beliefs. For example, a person may experience depression, fatigue, and weight gain from milk and wheat allergies. These symptoms incorrectly diagnosed may lead to unsuccessful treatment with counseling or drugs. If this person tries a diet free of milk and wheat, the clearing of symptoms experienced within one week will strongly reinforce a positive attitude change: "I know this isn't all in my head, some kind of subconscious negativity. I can do something about these problems." In addition, the discipline involved in following an allergen-free diet reinforces a healthy attitude that says: "I care about myself."

This cookbook and her previous *GOING AGAINST THE GRAIN* are a result of Phyllis' efforts to overcome her own health problems. Writing as an insider, she brings insight into what it takes to succeed at making a serious diet change. She shows us how to prepare healthy allergen-free foods easily, quickly, and economically. She gives us the tools to produce the textures and flavors we seek in breads and pastries. She teaches us creativity in working with substitutions, so that those who have multiple food allergies can accommodate their special needs. She helps us to really care for ourselves by eating aesthetic, healthy, satisfying food. Remember the old aphorism: "If I don't care for my body, where will I live?" May you each discover the highest level of health for yourself.

John A. Green M.D.

Aurora, Oregon

Contents

FOREWORD...vii

INTRODUCTION...xi

BREAD... 1

CAKES...73

PIES..103

COOKIES...127

MAIN COURSE...149

SOUPS...169

SAUCES...177

SWEETS...199

MISCELLANEOUS.....................................223

INDEX..251

INTRODUCTION

One of the most exciting days of my life was the day CNN came to my house! The Cable News Network was interested in knowing more about people who were sensitive to wheat and they were interested in the fact that I was publishing *Going Against the Grain Wheat-Free Cookery* all by myself on the dining room table! Caroline O'Neil, from *On the Menu* was here for 3 hours. (My first comment to her at the door was, "Thank goodness you're here. Now I can stop cleaning!!) She was such a friendly, professional lady. The resulting avalanche of calls from all over the country, Canada, New Zealand and the Virgin Islands, was totally unexpected. And time after time, people were asking me for bread recipes and preferably bread recipes that could be made in a bread machine! That is the reason for this book.

Many of the people who called or wrote to me were gluten intolerant and they were pleased with my combination of rice and bean flours, because this is a combination that they could safely use. However, since I am not gluten intolerant, I do have a few recipes which use other grains than wheat - which are to be avoided by the gluten intolerant. If you even suspect that you may have a gluten problem, avoid oats, rye, barley, wheat, millet, spelt, and kamut.

WHAT IS MY FOCUS?

Most of us need to discover and work with our food sensitivities. Allergy specialist, Dr. John A. Green of Aurora, Oregon encourages people who don't know why they feel ill to try wheat and dairy-free recipes for a few weeks to see if this makes a difference. Those of us who are aware of the foods that we need to avoid in order to feel well unfortunately tend to focus on the negative rather than on the positive. Eating becomes a chore when the list of negative foods for us becomes a long one. It is downright depressing to be told that you have to cut out bread, hamburger rolls, hot dogs, pancakes, pies, cookies, cakes, pizza, and, indeed everything we ever enjoyed eating. And every social occasion includes eating. We are invited to teas, desserts, pot lucks, happy hours, weddings and funerals...all have wonderful things that we cannot eat.

> "Eating is not merely a material pleasure. Eating well gives a spectacular joy to life and contributes immensely to goodwill and happy companionship. It is of great importance to the morale."

> Elsa Schiaparelli - Shocking Life, 1954

My purpose is to present truly delicious wheat-free recipes in a manner that sparks an enthusiasm for cooking and eating without the ingredients which cause some of us problems. This book makes good eating attainable for those who are having to change their eating habits. It is easier on the cook, who is trying to keep everyone happy, to eliminate the need for separate foods for family members. Everyone will enjoy these wheat-free recipes!

About the recipes...

This longing for good foods is what has prompted me to choose recipes for their "country good" background. These are the older treasured family recipes that have been modified to accommodate those of us who cannot eat wheat. Substitutions are made for milk as well. While I have tried to look for dairy and egg-free recipes I do use these ingredients in a few recipes, but you usually have some options. (See the section on ingredients, pg.xv). It is very difficult to write a cookbook addressing everyone's individual sensitivities, so I expect we all will have to do a little adapting or experimenting.

So many of us are working people who have so little time, it seems, for cooking. How do we cope with all this extra cooking for special diets? There are suggestions here for making the cook's job more time efficient. The emphasis is on simple recipes, although there are a couple of recipes that require more time, but they are so special and so good that one might want to consider them for very special occasions. There are recipes for mixes which can be stored or frozen, thus cutting down on preparation time. There is a little repetition of recipes from the first book, because I keep discovering more ways to use the "Biscuit Mix", so you see it again. The same applies to the pie crust and noodle recipes.

Considering equipment...

I have met many people having a diversity of breadmaking machines who all have had success making wheat-free breads, but you will need to make adjustments to your recipes. See more about breadmakers in the bread chapter. The pluses for a bread machine are that a machine is a great time and energy saver, (it doesn't heat up your kitchen), and there is little mess.

A food processor or blender is almost essential. They are so time efficient, and do a superior job of mixing and pureeing.

Baking dishes should be heavier metal or glass, never foil pans. It is recommended that oven temperatures be lowered by 25° if you are using glass.

Just because I have never been able to roll out a crust without a pastry cloth and stocking (rolling pin cover), I heartily recommend these items.

A timer that roars and stomps about the kitchen is essential!

A freezer can be an expensive investment, but one can often find an older used model if convenience and time are important enough considerations.

Not a necessity, but certainly helpful with non-wheat breads is an electric knife...something that one can often find at a garage sale.

Considering ingredients...

GLUTEN

When wheat flour is mixed with liquid and warmed, the gluten expands to form elastic strands capable of trapping bubbles of gas released by the yeast. This entrapment is what makes the bread rise. Without gluten, the bread is heavier and it does not stick together. If you need to avoid gluten, you need to avoid not only wheat, but oats, rye, barley, spelt, kamut, buckwheat, quinoa, and millet as they all contain some gluten.

FLOURS

Most of the recipes in this book are grain-free with heavy emphasis on rice and chickpea (garbanzo bean) flour combinations. You will find that wheat-free baked products usually require longer and slower baking. It is suggested that you do not open the oven door during baking, and that you allow baked goods to cool gradually before handling. This is where the electric knife is helpful in keeping the bread or cake from flattening.

Most of the flours mentioned in this book can be readily purchased at health food stores and some can be found in stores which carry bulk foods, notably those in ethnic areas. I am able to purchase rice and garbanzo (chickpea) flours in downtown Portland in an older area market which caters to its ethnic population, plus Portland has a mill which produces all of the flours you could ever need! It is desirable to fresh-mill whole grain flours or at least make every effort to buy them fresh-milled. I've been told to keep them in the freezer, but have had good luck keeping them in the refrigerator in a cellophane or plastic bag with the air squeezed out.

If you are of a mind to do some experimenting with alternative flours, you might consult *The Allergy Self Help Cookbook* by Marjorie Hurt Jones, RN. It is published by Rodale. The tables on cooking and baking with alternative flours are excellent.

XANTHAN GUM

You will need other ingredients to make your baked goods stick together. Xanthan gum is found in health food stores and is used extensively for holding baked goods together. Eggs will accomplish the same thing, but too many eggs presents other dangers, and people are seldom sensitive to Xanthan gum.

It is somewhat pricey, but a little seems to go a long way. I usually use 1 teaspoon Xanthan gum to each cup of flour.

If Xanthan gum is not available to you, you may substitute powdered pectin, (the kind you use to make jam) by substituting 1 teaspoon powdered pectin for each teaspoon Xanthan gum. The texture and taste will be slightly different, but still very good. Pectin keeps breads, cakes, cookies, etc. from being crumbly. If all you have on hand is liquid pectin, you can use that, also. Start off by trying 1 teaspoon liquid pectin for each teaspoon Xanthan gum asked for in the recipe. If you need to make your own pectin, there is a recipe for this; however, you may need to experiment with how much to add to each cup of flour.

YEAST

One packet of dry yeast = one yeast cake = one tablespoon dry yeast. You should keep the yeast in your refrigerator, and bring to room temperature before using. 1 tablespoon yeast will raise as much as 8 cups of flour. Dry yeast is much more stable than yeast cakes, lasting as long as a year in refrigeration. For testing the liveliness of your yeast, see pg. 5 in the bread section.

SUGAR

I have consciously tried to choose recipes requiring lesser amounts of sugar. Sugar gives structure and lightness to a breadlike recipe, so a recipe using honey may taste very good, but you will have a heavier baked product.

Some sweetener is necessary in your bread recipes to make your yeast raise. (BE CAREFUL: Too much sugar will kill the yeast.)

You can substitute for the sugar with honey or molasses, rice syrup or maple syrup. Honey may be substituted for sugar in most recipes without any liquid adjustments. Use 1/2 the amount of sugar called for, in honey, and lower the cooking temperature by 25°.

SALT

Salt keeps the yeast from running amuck. Too much salt will kill the yeast in your bread recipes.

SHORTENING

If you have to avoid gluten, you need to avoid hydrogenated shortening as well. So your choices for bread making would be oils, butter, or lard. Lard is recommended for giving a quality and texture not found with other shortenings. You usually use less, and the taste is worth it, but being animal fat, it is not something you should use extensively.

If it is not a problem, you may prefer to use butter as it adds immeasurably to the taste, but margarine or shortening can be substituted for the butter in all of these recipes. Read the labels to be sure you are using a product you can tolerate. Dr. Green warns of using margarine and shortening as they contain "trans fatty acids" which are not particularly good for you!

BAKING SODA

Never use baking soda that has been used as a deodorizer in your refrigerator, because its effectiveness will be reduced by moisture and odor. Add a spoonful of soda to a spoonful of vinegar in a dish. If it bubbles, it's still active. Generally, use baking soda with something acidic like buttermilk, applesauce, etc.

BAKING POWDER

To test your baking powder's effectiveness, put a teaspoon of the product in 1/4 cup warm water. If bubbles form on the surface, the product is still good. You can expect it to last about a year. If you want to avoid using products with aluminum salts, you can make your own. (Or visit your health food store!)

Mix 1 part corn starch, 1 part cream of tartar, and 1⁄2 part baking soda or,

Mix 1 part arrowroot, 1 part cream of tartar, and 1⁄2 part baking soda.

Mix very well and store in an air tight container. If recipe calls for 1 teaspoon regular baking powder, substitute 1 1⁄2 to 1 3⁄4 teaspoons homemade baking powder.

The average use of baking powder is 2 1⁄2 tsp baking powder to each cup of wheat-free flour.

Usually, use baking powder with sweet milk, never buttermilk.

When using this type of baking powder, do not allow your batter to stand long before it is baked, since the gas is given off the moment liquid is introduced. Get it mixed, into the pans and into the oven posthaste. Don't even answer the telephone until it's in the oven!

EGG REPLACER

I.   Soak 1⁄2 lb. APRICOTS in 2 cups water overnight. Next morning beat or blend them (add water if needed), strain them and store in refrigerator. Everytime your recipe calls for beaten eggs take a generous tablespoon of this and blend in your dough.

II.   To 3 cups of cold WATER add 1 cup ground FLAXSEED. Bring to a boil stirring constantly. Boil for 3 minutes. Cool. Place in the refrigerator in a closed jar. Whenever your recipe calls for 1 beaten egg, substitute 1 tbl. of above mixture, for 2 eggs take 2 tbl and so on. You can make all brands of pancakes, muffins, cookies, by substituting this recipe for the eggs.

III.   1 1/2 tablespoons WATER
        1 1/2 tablespoons OIL   makes 1 egg
        1 tsp BAKING POWDER

This recipe is courtesy of Kathy Forsyth, Mt. Lebanon, PA.

MILK SUBSTITUTES

Health food stores and many large grocery stores carry soy milk, almond milk and rice milk. Your health food store may also carry other nut milks or you can make them by processing 1/2 cup nuts (almonds and cashews are good choices) or seeds (sunflower) in 2 cup water blending until creamy. All will taste good on cereal and in any of this book's recipes, but water works also. When you substitute for milk in a breadlike recipe, you sacrifice lightness. A recipe which calls for milk, will be heavier with juice or water as a substitute, but it can be just as tasty.

MEASURING TIPS

I never knew there was a difference
between a liquid measuring cup and
a dry measuring cup. To tell the truth,
I do not think that it makes much difference
which you use - **most** of the time.
However, when you are measuring
dry ingredients for bread, in particiular,
it is good to abide by the following
instructions:

1. Use a multi-cup measure for liquid
   measurements.

2. Use an exact cup (or 1/2, 1/3, or 1/4
   cup) measure for dry ingredients,**tap**
   the side of the measuring cup a couple
   of times with a straight-edge knife and
   level it off by running the knife over the
   top of the cup.

Never use the measuring cup as a scoop. It
will pack too much flour thus affecting your
accuracy.

A few words about allergies...

No one can help you as well as a doctor whose area of expertise is food allergies. If you have food allergies or sensitivities, you need to be aware of the need for food rotation. Eating the same foods day after day can bring about sensitivities to those foods. Thus you cannot become dependent upon oat or corn flour and use it in all your baked goods, because you *can* become sensitive to those grains as well. To be on the safe side, you should try to rotate your food choices so as to not eat a grain or sensitive food more often than once every 2-4 days. This is where your freezer comes in. Remember when you make a pan of Amish Friendship Bread, dole out servings for everyone at the table. Then divide the rest into lunch size servings, freeze in plastic bags or wrap and label, thus making very handy snacks to take with you when you need "fast food." Some people even have special shelves in their freezers for food rotation. Keep a shelf or container labeled "oat", "corn", "rice", or "bean" flours. On day 1, you eat from shelf #1. On day 2, you eat from shelf #2 and so on. Dr. John Green says rotation should keep foods of the same group at least 2 days apart, so you may want to skip a day between rice/garbanzo products and have no grain or legumes in between. Some people can get away with eating grain daily." But he cautions, "I see much rice sensitivity from over-dosing on rice."

With everything packaged and labeled, you can grab a muffin and take it with you to that breakfast meeting. You can always have something delicious whenever everyone else is going for the donut.

FLOUR SUBSTITUTIONS

1 cup of wheat flour equals...

- 7/8 cup amaranth
- 7/8 cup bean (garbanzo bean)
- 7/8 cup buckwheat
- 3/4 cup chickpea (garbanzo)
- 3/4 cup corn flour
- 1 cup corn meal
- 3/4 cup millet flour
- 3/4 cup oat flour
- 5/8 cup potato flour
- 3/4 cup potato starch
- 7/8 cup rice flour
- 3/4 cup soy flour
- 1 cup tapioca flour

BEWARE of using one or two flours exclusively. Almost everyone can tolerate rice flour, but you can develop a sensitivity to any food if you overdo its usage.

See Rodales' *The Allergy Self-Help Cookbook* by Marjorie Hurt Jones, RN, for a comprehensive explanation of alternative flours.

BREAD

"Climb the mountains
and get their good tidings;
Nature's peace will flow into you
as sunshine into flowers;
the winds will blow their freshness
into you
and the storms their energy,
and cares will drop off
like autumn leaves."

John Muir

A LOT TO DO ABOUT BREAD MACHINES!

I was never able to make a decent loaf of bread, and for most of my life, there was no need for me to learn. If you have to avoid wheat or perhaps all grains, you will only get good bread if you make it yourself! So, the bread machine is a godsend. And yes, you can make wheat-free bread in a machine with very little effort. I do not consider myself an expert, but here is what I have learned.

All bread machines employ the same principles. The ingredients are combined in a single canister, mixed and kneaded mechanically, and then baked in the same canister. There are many manufacturers of bread machines, but they seem to fall into two categories; the first category contains the machines in which you start with the dry yeast added to the bottom of your bread canister, followed by the dry ingredients, then the liquid ingredients. You push a button and the machine does the rest. Both the small and large size Welbilt work on this principle.

The second category contains the machines in which you add the liquid ingredients first, then the dry ingredients and lastly, you sprinkle the yeast over the top of the dry ingredients. When you are baking wheat-free, you need to **change** the order in this second category. Mix all ingredients together in a bowl and **then** spoon the dough into the bread canister. Then, you push a button and the machine does its work. The dough is just too heavy to work well if you do not mix it first. The Zojirushi, the Dak,

Panasonic, and the Hitachi work on this principle. You cannot use the feature that starts your breadmaking while you are away or asleep, as your yeast will already be moistened and you run the risk that it does not work well for you.

To avoid disappointments, it is important not to interchange the methods used in category one and two.

If you wish to adapt your machine's recipes to wheat-free, be prepared for some trial and error loaves. *Sunset Magazine* did a very comprehensive article on "How to Make Bread Machines Work for You" by Betsy Reynolds Bateson, which states that "Recipes from general bread machine cookbooks are not usually developed for a particular machine and may work better in some machines than others." So you have some experimenting to do!

A few machines have a heat-up period before mixing, so you don't have to worry about temperature, but many machines require that the ingredients are room-temperature and some say liquids need to be 75°-110°. Yeast works best at 85°. Below 75° slows down the yeast's action and over 120° will kill the yeast.

"Machines can't compensate for variations in humidity, heat, altitude, and ingredients. That's why they sometimes produce overproofed loaves, loaves that don't rise properly, and loaves that are doughy—and why a recipe that's successful in spring and fall may not work as well in summer."

Keep track of changes you make, so that next time you can build on your experience and you can keep track of what is working for you. Stay with your machine's flour capacity. One ingredient you will not need to change is the yeast. "If a loaf fails to work after you've experimented with the liquid and flour, you can change (one at a time) the other ingredients that affect rising...yeast, salt, sugar, and fat."

Check to make sure your yeast is still good. (Keep it in the refrigerator.) Test your yeast by adding a pinch of yeast to a little warm water and 1/2 teaspoon of sugar or honey. If it bubbles and foams, it is working.

"Salt retards yeast's action, so you may want to decrease it by half. Or, there might not be enough sugar to feed the yeast. Try increasing the sugar by 50%. If that doesn't work, reduce the fat—it also slows yeast's action.'"

I have heard it said that it is better to get a bread maker that has the mixer blade at the bottom of the cannister as wheat-free dough tends to sit heavily on the bottom. You may want to experiment with the recipes that come with your machine, but the proportions of flour and liquid have to be adjusted as in the recipes that follow. As I have said before, the pluses for a bread machine are that a machine is a great time and energy saver, and the bread is very good.

On the following pages are listed some bread-making problems and possible solutions. Try one suggestion at a time. Take notes on what works and what doesn't.

1. Betsy Reynolds Bateson, "How to Make Bread Machines Work for You," *Sunset   Magazine.* October, 1993, pg 162.

BREAD MACHINE PROBLEMS

(Remember, try one suggestion at a time.)

Problem #1

Sunken middle (adjust the flour-liquid ratio)

First, try increasing the flour.

Then try decreasing the sugar.

Problem #2

Bread rises too high, then sinks

First try decreasing the liquid.

Then try decreasing the sugar by 50%

Try decreasing the yeast by 25%.

Then try decreasing the fat by 50%.

Problem #3

Large uneven holes   (leavening action is too fast)

First, decrease liquid.

Then try decreasing yeast.

Try using regular active dry yeast, rather than rapid or quick yeast.

Then try increasing the salt by 50%.

Problem #4

Looks like "Big Foot"   (too much flour)

Try reducing the flour.

Then increase the yeast.

Try increasing the liquid, but not so much that recipe becomes too large for machine.

Problem #5

Too dense (Inadequate gluten or inefficient leavening)

Try substituting a finer flour (perhaps 1/4 - 1/2 cup potato starch or tapioca flour) for some of the flour.

Then try increasing the yeast and/ or sugar.

You may also substitute some hops tea for the liquid.   (Pg.12)

Try 1 teaspoon liquid lecithin.

Try pulverizing a calcium tablet and adding this to your batter.

This is probably how most of your loaves without gluten, eggs or milk will look, but they can still be tasty!!

This information is based on a *Sunset Magazine* article by Betsy Reynolds Bateson, March 1993.

MANUAL BREAD MAKING

The dough for a bread machine tends to be stickier - like a very heavy batter. But you can still use these bread machine recipes to make bread manually. Just add enough extra flour to make the dough easy to work with. This is something you need to experiment with by sprinkling your dough and hands with flour until it is no longer sticky.

When a recipe instructs you to knead the dough for one minute after the first rising period, before making a loaf or rolls, **do not** add flour. Knead the dough in its container. What you are doing is moving the sweetener around so that the yeast has a new food source.

After you have kneaded the dough for a few minutes and the dough is soft and silky smooth to the touch but **not** sticky, it is ready for its first rising.

If your recipe asks you to oil the top of the dough before rising, do it gently with your fingertips.

Most recipes will tell you to let the dough raise until it is double in bulk. A wheat-free loaf will not double in size..more like it will rise 1/2 its bulk. Experience will tell how long that will take. It is usually a little longer than with wheat flours. When it has risen 1/2 again its bulk, it is ready to be punched down and to go on to the next direction.

When shaping the loaf for the second rising, handle it gently, as if it were fragile.

When the bread is done baking, it should sound hollow if tapped with your fingers or a knife. If you are like me, you will be wondering, "So, what does hollow sound like?' or "Does that sound hollow enough?" Experience, they tell me, is the best teacher in this case!

Helpful hints: If it is difficult to find a warm place to let your bread dough rise, consider setting dough in a covered bowl on top of an electric heating pad turned on low. The ideal temperature for yeast to multiply is 82°-85°.

Immediately remove loaves from pans when they are done and lay on their sides on wire racks to cool. Fresh bread slices better when cool, unless you are using an electric knife. When cool, slice unused portion, package tightly, label and freeze. If you are rotating your foods, the labeling is important.

There are so many good things to do with your "not so successful" experiments with bread. Save your leftovers for recipes like "Stewed bread" (pg.166) or to make stuffings for the turkey!

Erica Calkins, Heritage Food Specialist in Oregon City, gives this helpful hint from the pages of history, for our breadmaking. HOPS TEA encourages the rising of yeast breads and is easy to make.

HOPS TEA

3-4 flower heads   1/2 cup boiling water

Three or four flower heads from the hops plant steeped in a half cup of boiling water will give enough tea to be included as part of the liquid in your bread recipes. Breads are noticeably higher and more flavorful with the tea.

Also the hops were used as a preservative in the "old days" giving bread a sponginess. If you have access to hops, give them a try.

"Manna" from heaven!! SPELT is a grain used in biblical times. It is a variety of wheat which some wheat-sensitive people can tolerate while others cannot. You will be the best judge. (If GLUTEN is your problem, you will want to avoid spelt.)

For the 1 pound loaf for the Welbilt-type breadmaking machine...

SPELT BREAD

1 tbl dried yeast	1 tbl oil
2 tbl granulated sugar	2 eggs
1/2 tsp salt	1 tsp cider or
2 cups spelt flour	wine vinegar*

PLACE yeast and sugar together in one corner of
    the baking cannister.

ADD salt and spelt flour.

POUR eggs, oil, and vinegar in a measuring cup.

GENTLY FILL this cup with warm water to 1 cup
    plus 2 more tablespoons warm water. (110°-
    115°) and add to bread cannister.

PUSH START BUTTON and use the basic bread
    setting.

YOU ARE FREE TO DIDDLE AROUND FOR 2
    HOURS AND 15 MINUTES!

*Clear vinegar is made from grains and should be
avoided.

If you have the kind of breadmaker that requires the
liquid be added first, combine and mix all ingredients well, and add the dough to your bread cannister.

You can also use your own familiar manual
breadmaking skills with this recipe. See page 10.

For the Zojirushi-type breadmaker which makes a 1 1/2 pound loaf*...

"Manna" from heaven!! SPELT is a grain used in biblical times. It is a variety of wheat which some wheat-sensitive people can tolerate while others cannot. You will be the best judge. (If GLUTEN is your problem, you will want to avoid spelt.)

SPELT BREAD

1 tbl yeast	1 cup water + 2 tbl
1 1/2 tbl honey	3 cups spelt flour
1 1/2 tbl canola oil	1 tsp salt

COMBINE honey , oil, and water.

ADD flour, yeast, and salt to the honey mixture.

PUT into the bread cannister.

PUSH start button and you are free as a bird!!

*If you have the kind of breadmaker that requires the yeast and dry ingredients to be added first, follow the directions on page 3.

You can also use your own familiar manual breadmaking skills with this recipe. See page 10.

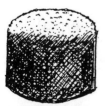

A BREAD FLOUR MIX

To simplify your life, try making a mix of the dry flour ingredients you need to use in your bread making. It is always best to use at least 2 or 3 types of flour in your recipe.

8 cups garbanzo bean flour	8 tbl Xanthan
12 cups rice flour (brown or white)	gum
4 cups potato starch or tapioca flour	2 1/2 tbl salt
	1 cup sugar

If your bread recipe calls for 3 cups of flour, use 3 cups plus 3 tablespoons of your mix. REMEMBER you have included salt, sugar and gum in your flour measurement, so you have the extra 3 tablespoons of the mix.

If your recipe calls for 2 cups of flour, use 2 cups plus 2 1/2 tablespoons of your mix. Again remember that you have included the salt, sugar, and gum in your flour measurement, so you have the extra 2 1/2 tablespoons of the mix.

You may substitute the following for the bean flour: white bean, corn, oat, rye, or millet flours. If you must avoid **gluten** you need to **avoid** the oat, rye, and millet.

For the Zojirushi-type breadmaker which makes a
1 1/2 pound loaf* . . .

*KAMUT (pronounced Kah-mut) is another ancient
grain. According to Arrowhead Mills, Kamut Flour
"contains a unique type of gluten easier for your body
to utilize than common wheat." Ask your doctor. If
you are GLUTEN-intolerant, you will want to avoid
Kamut.*

KAMUT BREAD

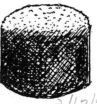

2/17/95

1 tbl yeast	1 1/2 tbl honey
3 cups kamut flour	1 1/2 tbl oil
1/2 tsp salt	1 cup water + 6 tbl

used a little less water

COMBINE yeast, flour, and salt. *& added 2 TBLS flour while kneading because sticky*

COMBINE honey, oil, and water in a larger bowl.

ADD flour mixture to the honey mixture and mix well.

PUT into the bread canister.

PUSH start button and put your feet up!!

*If you have the kind of breadmaker that requires
the yeast and dry ingredients to be added first, follow the directions on page 3.

You can also use your own familiar manual
breadmaking skills with this recipe. However, cut the
liquid back to 1 1/4 cups for 3 cups flour. See page 10

for the Welbilt-type breadmaker, 1 pound loaf...

WALRUS BREAD

or "A loaf of bread is what we chiefly need." (Lewis Carroll - *Alice Through the Looking Glass.*)

1 tbl yeast	1 tbl oil
2/3 cup garbanzo bean flour*	1 tsp vinegar
1 cup rice flour	1 egg
1⁄3 cup potato starch	enough water to
1 1⁄2 tbl sugar	make 1 cup + 7
1 tsp salt	tbl
2 tsp Xanthan gum	

PLACE yeast in one corner of the bottom of the bread
     bucket.

MIX the rest of the dry ingredients in a large bowl.

ADD to the bread bucket. (*be sure the kneader is in
     the bucket!!)*

USING water from your hot water faucet, (about
     110-115°)...

COMBINE eggs, oil, vinegar and water to make 1
     cup + 7 tbl of liquid and pour over the dry
     mixture.

SET controls for medium setting and press START.
     (*I usually get bread about 3 1⁄2 - 4" high.)*

CURL up with something you've been meaning to
    read!!

*You may substitute 1 cup white bean flour, 1 cup
corn flour, or 1 cup oat flour.

This recipe can be used in the conventional breadmaking way. Just follow the directions in your own
cookbooks.

for the Zojirushi-type bread maker - 1 1/2 pound loaf...

WALRUS BREAD

or "A loaf of bread is what we chiefly need." (Lewis
Carroll - *Alice Through the Looking Glass.*)

1 cup garbanzo bean flour*	2 eggs
1 1/2 cup rice flour (brown or white)	2 tbl oil
1/2 cup potato starch	1 tsp vinegar
3 tsp Xanthan gum	1 3/4 cup water
1 tsp salt	
2 tbl sugar	
1 tbl yeast	

MIX the 7 dry ingredients in a large bowl.

USING water from your hot water faucet, (about
        110-115°)...

MIX eggs, oil, vinegar and water in a separate bowl
and add to the dry mixture.

MIX until well-moistened.

SPOON into the bread maker bucket. (*be sure the
kneader is in the bucket!!*)

SET controls for basic white bread and lite setting.
(*I usually get bread about 5 inches high.*)

CURL up with something you've been meaning to
read!!

*You may substitute 1 cup white bean flour, 1 cup
corn flour, or 1 cup oat flour.

This recipe can be used in the conventional breadmaking way. Just follow the directions in your own
cookbooks.

*Once you get your basic bread recipe the way you
want it, you might like to try some of the following
combinations to vary the flavor.*

SEASONING THE BREAD

For a 1 1/2 pound loaf try...

1 tsp celery flakes
1 tsp dried sage
1/3 cup dried minced onion

1/3 cup hulled millet
1/2 tsp liquid lecithin
3/4 cup raw sunflower
    seeds

or

or

1/2 tsp liquid lecithin
2 tsp caraway seeds
1 tsp dried dill weed

1/4 cup dried minced
    onion

or

or

1 tsp vanilla
1/4 cup raisins
1/4 cup dates
1/4 cup walnuts
1 tsp cinnamon

3 tbl quinoa grain
1/3 cup sesame seeds

or

or

1 tsp aniseed
1 tsp caraway
grated zest of 1 1/2 oranges

3 tbl minced dried onion
1 tbl caraway seeds

or

or

to 3 cups of flour and
    3/4 cup liquid
add 1/2 cup liquid egg
    substitute

1/4 tsp cardamom
1/4 cup chopped
    dates
3 tbl chopped dried
    apricots(cont.)

or   1/3 cup chopped
                                          dried apples
1/4 tsp fennel seed   1 tsp cinnamon
1/2 tsp grated orange peel   lemon zest (1 1/2
                                          lemons)
                                      1 large egg (2 tsp
                                          liquid egg
                                          substitute)

*For 1 pound loaves, use 2/3 of these measurements.

Barley flour makes great bread but if gluten is a problem, avoid barley.

BARLEY BREAD

1 tbl yeast   1/3 cup bean flour
2 tsp brown sugar   1 tbl oil
1 cup warm water   1 tsp salt
2 cups barley flour

PUT yeast into a small bowl.

ADD 1/2 tsp of the brown sugar and 1/2 cup of warm
        water.

PUT into a warm place to raise.

PUT remaining 1⁄2 cup warm water into large mixing bowl.

ADD 1 cup of flour and mix vigorously.

ADD rest of the brown sugar, the oil, and salt and mix well.

ADD softened yeast and beat briskly,

ADD bean flour and enough barley flour to make dough that can be kneaded.

PLACE on floured board and KNEAD until smooth and elastic.

SHAPE into two round loaves on cookie sheet and slash diagonally.

LET rise until double in bulk and oil top lightly if desired.

BAKE at 350° for one hour.

REMOVE from pans and cool on rack.

Bud and Jean Clem of Western Trails, Inc. of Bozeman, Montana, 59715, contributed this information and this excellent bread recipe.

_Dr. D. W. Thom, DDS, ND, of the Portland
Naturopathic Clinic, here in Oregon shares this recipe
with us._

SWEET WHEATLESS BREAD

2 tsp dry yeast
2-3 tbl honey
1/3 cup lukewarm water
1 cup brown rice flour
1 1/2 cup rye flour
1 cup oat flour

2 tsp cinnamon
(optional)
1/2 cup raisins (optional)
1 3/4 cup boiling water
2 tbl canola oil
2 tsp sea salt

ADD the honey to the 1/3 cup lukewarm water.

DISSOLVE dry yeast in this mixture and set aside.

COMBINE rice, oat, and rye flours with spice and
raisins.

COMBINE boiling water, salt, and oil in electric mixer
bowl and add to the flour mixture.

COOL till lukewarm.

ADD yeast mixture and beat for 2-3 minutes.

(This can also be done by hand.)

PLACE smooth dough in a greased bowl.

COVER bowl with damp cloth and set in larger bowl
of hot water to rise for 2 hours.

BEAT dough again for 2-3 minutes.

TURN dough into oiled 9" x 5" x 3" loaf pan.

SET in unheated oven to rise for 40-45 minutes or
    until dough has just reached the top of the
    pan.

TURN oven on to 400° and let bread bake for 10
    minutes.

TURN heat down to 325° and bake for 40-45 min
    utes longer.

TURN loaf out of pan and cool on a rack before
    slicing.

NOTE: Spice and raisins can be omitted for a plainer,
but still delicious loaf. For this, use 2 tablespoons of
honey.

Yield: 1 loaf

For the 1 1/2 pound bread machine, a flavorful rye
bread.*

HIGH FIVE RYE BREAD

2-3 tbl honey   2 tsp cinnamon
1 3/4 cup lukewarm water   1/2 tsp anise seeds
1 tbl canola oil   2 tsp instant coffee
2 tsp cider or wine vinegar   granules
1 cup brown rice flour   2 tbl cocoa
1 1/2 cup rye flour   2 tbl caraway seeds
1 cup oat flour   (optional)
1 tsp Xanthan gum   1/2 cup raisins (optional)
1 tsp sea salt
1 tbl + 1 tsp yeast

COMBINE honey, water, and oil and set aside.

COMBINE flours, gum, salt, yeast, spice, seeds,
       coffee,and cocoa.

ADD liquid ingredients to the dry ingredients and mix
       well.

SPOON into the bread maker bucket. (*be sure the
       kneader is in the bucket!!*)

BAKE at longest cycle or at the basic white bread,
medium cycle. If your machine cannot bake for a
long enough time to cook the bread all the way
through, try baking it conventionally in the oven
at 300° for 2 hours.

ADD raisins when your bread machine indicates.

PUT your feet up with a good book...or just watch
      the grass grow!!

TURN loaf out of bread bucket when done and cool
      on a rack before slicing.

*This recipe should work for any machine which
specifies adding liquids first & dry ingredients last.

GUIDELINES FOR MAINTAINING A SWEET SPIRIT WHILST WORKING WITH **SOUR DOUGH**

Researching the subject of sourdough baking is like climbing a mountain, only everybody is climbing a different mountain! Since there are so many ways to make starter, and "feed" it and use it, I will try to take the easiest way...certainly not the only way.

WHAT EQUIPMENT YOU NEED:
Start with a jar or crock that will hold at least 1/2 gallon of liquid. You can cover the crock or jar with cloth or plastic or a pottery lid; just be sure you do not let the contents of the jar come in contact with metal.

MAKING THE "STARTER":
You will need to add the following to your jar:

> 2 cups warm water (no more than 115° F for dried yeast or 90°F for yeast cake)
> 1 tablespoon dry powdered yeast (or one yeast cake)
> 2 cups rice flour
> 1 teaspoon sugar

ALLOW to sit at room temperature until fermented and bubbly - about 15 minutes in a warm room. Dr. Green encourages the use of natural "wild" yeasts, but I have not worked with them.

WHEN bubbly and slightly risen, cover and refrigerate. Some say starter should always be stored in a refrigerator. Others say to keep starter at room temperature for 5 days, stirring each morning and using on the 6th day. THEN refrigerate. Still others say, "Let the starter stand in a warm position for 30 minutes then store in the fridge until needed, but wait 24 hours before using. I think what you do depends on just how sour you like your baked goods to be. The longer the starter stands on your counter, the stronger the sour taste.

YOUR SCHEDULE:

Day #1	Put your starter ingredients together and cover.
Day #2,3,4,	Stir with a wooden spoon.
Day #5,	**FEED THE STARTER** 1 cup flour 1 cup warm water 1 tsp sugar COVER loosely with cloth or plastic. Let rest for 24 hours.
Day #6	Take out the amount of starter you need for your recipe. Replace what you've taken (by feeding it) and continue with your baking...

ALWAYS bring up to room temperature before using. Most sourdough baking failures occur because the basic batter was kept too cool the night before baking.

SO... you bring it up to room temperature, (if refrigerated) use it and continue, always remembering to replace what you've taken.

REPLACE THE STARTER

> 1 cup flour
> 1 cup warm water
> 1 tsp sugar

> COVER loosely with cloth or plastic.
> Let rest for 24 hours.

IF starter becomes too sour, simply add a pinch of baking soda to sweeten it.

Water, warmth, and a teaspoon of sweetener, (sugar, honey, fructose) will bring the starter back to life, if it's gone dry.

Test your yeast by adding a pinch of sugar and a teaspoon warm water to about a tablespoon of starter. If it bubbles and foams, it is working.

It might be fun to try an old fashioned starter...

> 1 large potato boiled in 1 pint of water until
>   mushy
> 1 tablespoon dry yeast or 1 yeast cake
> 1/4 cup sugar

MASH potato well.

POUR potato, yeast, and sugar into a quart jar.

SET out at room temperature until it is bubbling and
lively.

COVER and refrigerate.

AMISH FRIENDSHIP BREAD

*This is a revised traditional recipe adapted from The
Small Farm Journal, Winter 1991.*

1 cup starter	1 cup sugar
2/3 cup oil	1 tsp cinnamon
3 eggs	2 tsp baking powder
1 tsp vanilla	1/2 tsp baking soda
1 cup rice flour	1/2 tsp salt
7/8 cup bean flour	

Optional: 1/4 cup chopped citron
              1/4 cup chopped glaced cherries
                    or
              1/2 cup raisins
                    or
              1/2 cup chopped nuts
                    or
              Whatever suits your pleasure!!!

MIX dry ingredients.

ADD any of the optional items to the dry ingredients, coating them well.

ADD to the liquid ingredients.

POUR into a greased and floured loaf pan.

BAKE 60 minutes at 300°.

These pancakes are so easy to take on a picnic and are so good, you don't even have to tell anyone they're wheat-free.

SOURDOUGH PANCAKES

3 cups starter   1 tsp soda
2 tbl sugar or honey   2 tbl warm water
1/4 tsp salt
1 egg, well beaten
1 tbl cooking oil

MIX first 5 ingredients together.

ADD 1/4 - 1/2 cup of any wheat-free flour, if batter is too thin.

JUST before baking, add the soda and warm water.
(Batter should foam up immediately.)

SPOON onto a hot griddle.

TURN each pancake and serve hot with your favorite toppings.

If you are working by hand...

SOURDOUGH BREAD

1 cup sourdough starter	2 cups rice flour
2 cups warm water	2 cups bean flour
2 tbl honey	4 tsp Xanthan gum
2 tsp salt	1 tbl yeast
2 tbl cooking oil	

TAKE your starter out the night before and let it sit
overnight.

MIX the first 5 ingredients together.

ADD the flours and gum and mix well. If dough is
sticky, add flour to your hands. Try not to add
too much flour to the dough.

COVER the dough and let it rise for about 4 hours or until it about doubles.

SHAPE the dough into 2 loaves, kneading just a little.

PUT into greased loaf pan or on a cookie sheet for a French loaf.

LET rise for a couple of hours until about doubled.

BAKE 60 minutes at 300°.

SOURDOUGH BREAD (for your Welbilt-type bread maker, 1 pound loaf)*

1 tsp yeast	1/2 cup sourdough
1 cup rice flour	starter
1 cup bean flour	1 cup + 1 tbl warm
2 tsp Xanthan gum	water
1 tsp salt	1 tbl oil
1 1/2 tbl sugar or 1 tbl honey	

TAKE your starter out the night before and let it set over night.

PLACE the yeast in the corner of the bottom of your bread machine bucket.

MIX the flours, gum, salt and sugar, and add to the
    bucket *(Be sure the kneader is in the bucket!!)*

USING water from your hot water faucet, (about
    110-115°)...

COMBINE starter, water and oil.

ADD to the bread bucket.

SET for "dark setting".

PUT your feet up and write your best friend a letter!

*This recipe should work for any machine which
specifies dry ingredients first and liquids last.

SOURDOUGH BREAD (for your Zoshirushi-
        type bread maker - 1 1/2 pound loaf)*

1 tbl + 1/2 tsp yeast   3/4 cup sourdough
1 1/2 cup rice flour   starter
1 cup bean flour   about 1 1/2 cups warm
1/2 cup potato starch   water
3 tsp Xanthan gum   1 tbl oil
1 tsp salt
2 tbl sugar or 1 1/2 tbl honey

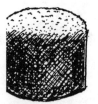

TAKE your starter out the night before and let it set
       overnight.

MIX dry ingredients together.

MIX starter, oil, and water in a large measuring cup
       to make 2 cups liquid.

ADD liquid ingredients to the dry ingredients and mix
       well.

PUT into the bread bucket of your machine.

SET for French bread setting. This is a longer set
       ting which is good for sourdough bread.

PUT up your feet and think good things about your
       self!

*This recipe should work for any machine which
specifies adding liquids first and dry ingredients last.*

We have to talk about BAGELS...

Most of my failures with bagels came about, I believe, because they need a **long** rising time and I
was judging them by wheat standards. So leave

them alone and be patient. I punched the dough down after 3 hours and put the covered bowl in the refrigerator for the night. Next morning, I formed the bagels, covered them, and left them in a cool kitchen until I came home at noon, at which time I placed them on a warm heating pad and went about my business. About 3 o'clock, they had risen about 1/2 an inch, so I proceeded with the boiling process. And then the baking...Husband, Ed, and I, armed with a small bag of 40 minute bagels and another of 50 minute bagels, sampled all the way to an evening auction we were attending.

"Hand me another of the 50 minute bagels," asks Ed.

"I like the 40 minute bagels," I reply.

"Too chewy," he says. "But not bad. Hand me one of those, too."

The upshot is that we could not decide, so that decision is left up to you!!

SOURDOUGH BAGELS

2 cups sourdough starter   3 tbl oil
2 cups rice flour   1/2 cup warm water
2 cups bean flour   2 tbl honey
4 tsp Xanthan gum   1 tbl yeast
1 tsp salt   Optional: 1 egg

Glaze: 1 egg white + 1 tbl cold water

COMBINE flours, gum, salt, and yeast and mix well.

ADD rest of the ingredients.

KNEAD until smooth and elastic.

COVER and let rise for 3 hours in a warm place in
  an oiled bowl. (a heating pad helps)

KNEAD again, gently, and roll out to 1/2" - 3/4" thickness. Try not to roll out too many times as
  the dough absorbs more flour each time and
  will get heavier.

CUT out or form bagel shapes on a lightly floured
  board. (I used a pineapple cutter!)

LET rise for about 2 hours or until you see about
  1/2" increase in height of the dough.

BOIL about 2 inches of water in a large pan.

ADD about 3 bagels at a time and simmer for 6 minutes.

TURN bagels over for about 1 more minute.

REMOVE from the water and place on a towel or
  cloth to cool.

COOL for 5 minutes.

PLACE bagels on ungreased baking sheets.

BRUSH tops with oil or egg white and water.

BAKE at 350° for 40-50 minutes. (See note at
        beginning of recipe.)

After a day or two, these are best warmed or toasted,
as they dry out quickly.

The fact that everyone measures a little differently,
everyone's sourdough starter will be slightly different, and given the humidity on a given day, you can
see that success might be illusive. Keep track of
what you do (If this is **your**book, you **can** write in
it!!!) and experiment with the amount of liquid that
you add to your batter. Try using hops tea if you
can. (See page12) I think it adds to the chewiness
and height.

If you want to experiment without using sourdough,
remember that the sourdough starter is 1 cup water
and 1 cup flour, so adjust your recipe accordingly.

This bread can be steamed or baked in your oven.
The steamed bread is more moist.

BROWN BREAD

1 1/2 cups bean flour	1/2 tsp salt
1 1/2 cups rye	2 cups buttermilk
1 cup corn meal	(or applesauce)
1/2 cup sugar	1 cup mild molasses
2 tsp soda	1 cup raisins

PREHEAT oven to 375°.

HAVE your ingredients all ready in order to get your
     bread into the oven quickly.

COMBINE flours, corn meal, and sugar.

MIX soda and salt into buttermilk or applesauce.

ADD to flour mixture.

ADD molasses and raisins.

GREASE about 5 cans (like a 16 oz fruit can).

POUR about 1 cup batter into each can.

BAKE 30 minutes or until cake tester comes out
     clean.

REMOVE from oven. COOL for 5 minutes.

REMOVE bread from cans. COOL on wire rack.

WRAP securely and store overnight in refrigerator
before serving.

or

COVER the cans tightly with foil and string. (rubber
bands work)

PLACE on a rack set in a large Dutch oven.

POUR boiling water in to depth of 1 inch.

COVER and simmer over low heat, steaming bread
till done. (2 1/2 - 3 hours)

ADD more boiling water as needed.

REMOVE bread from cans and cool on a rack.

Optional: You might want to add a teaspoon of
Xanthan gum if the bread is a bit too crumbly.

Amaranth flour has a distinctive flavor that goes well with fruit.

BROWN BREAD GRAIN-FREE

1 cup plus 2 tbl amaranth flour
1/4 cup arrowroot flour
1 tsp baking soda
1/2 tsp powdered ginger
1 tsp Xanthan gum

1/2 cup currants
    or chopped
    prunes
1/2 cup walnuts,
    almonds, or
    Brazil nuts
3/4 cup boiling
    water
1/4 cup honey or
    molasses
1 tbl lemon juice

GREASE a 1 quart mold or coffee can.

FILL a deep kettle or canner with about 5 inches of
        water.

BRING to a boil.

COMBINE the flour, arrowroot, baking soda, ginger,
        and gum in a bowl.

STIR in the currants.

GRIND the nuts to a powder in a blender or proces-
        sor.

ADD the water to the blender and blend.

ADD more water, if necessary, to the nuts and water
to make 1 cup of liquid.

ADD the honey or molasses and the lemon juice to
this liquid.

COMBINE the liquid mixture with the flour, stirring
quickly to blend. (Do not overmix.)

POUR into prepared mold.

COVER with foil or wax paper and tie securely with
a piece of string.

SET on a rack or jar rings in the kettle or canner.

ADD boiling water to canner until it reaches halfway
up sides of the mold.

COVER and steam for 2 hours, keeping water boiling gently.

REMOVE the mold from the pot.

COOL the bread about 15 minutes.

REMOVE from the mold onto a wire rack.

This is the kind of food that you keep in the freezer ready to be taken along for a business or social meeting...as good as anyone else will have! (Maybe better!)

BRAN LOAF

1 cup rice or corn bran	3⁄4 cup rice flour
1 cup raisins	3⁄4 cup bean flour
3⁄4 cup white sugar	1 1⁄2 tsp Xanthan gum
1 1⁄2 cup water	3 tsp baking powder

MIX bran, sugar, raisins, and water in bowl.

LET stand 2 hours or overnight.

ADD flour, gum and baking powder.

BAKE in greased loaf pan for 1 hour at 350°

    or

BAKE in muffin tin for 35 minutes at 325°.

FILL tins nearly full.

Makes 1 dozen

Summer's coming when you can pick strawberries at Bill Osmer's down the road in Canby. Pick enough for this lovely bread.

STRAWBERRY BREAD

2/3 cup rice flour	1 cup sugar
2/3 cup bean flour	2 eggs
1/2 tsp baking soda	1/2 cup vegetable oil
1 tsp Xanthan gum	12 oz fresh strawberries
1 tsp cinnamon	(a pint of fresh or
pinch of salt	about 1 1 /2 cup
	thawed.)
	1 tsp vanilla
	1/2 cup chopped nuts
	(walnuts are good)

SLICE and slightly mash strawberries and put aside.

COMBINE the first 6 ingredients and put aside.

BEAT sugar, eggs,and oil in a large bowl.

ADD flour mixture to the sugar mixture and mix
        quickly

FOLD in the strawberries, vanilla, and nuts.

POUR into a greased loaf pan and get it into the
        oven as quickly as you can.

BAKE at 325° for about ten minutes.

CONTINUE baking at 300° for about 1 hour and 35 minutes.

COOL.

Wonderful with coffee or a dessert wine or cheese. The eggs add richness, but you can omit them and add 1/3 cup water.

ITALIAN BISCUIT BREAD

1 cup butter or margarine   3/4 cup bean flour
1 cup sugar   3/4 cup rice flour
3 eggs   1 tsp xanthan gum
3 tbl sweet Marsala* wine   1/3 cup chopped dried
1 1/2 tsp vanilla extract   apricots
pinch salt   1/3 cup chopped dates
                                            1/3 cup chopped prunes
                                                or dried figs
                                            1/2 cup chopped roasted
                                                hazel nuts

COMBINE butter and sugar in large bowl.

ADD eggs, one at a time, beating well after each
        addition.

ADD Marsala, vanilla, and salt and set aside.

COMBINE flours and xanthan gum.

MIX dried fruits and nuts with flour mixture.

ADD to the batter.

POUR batter into greased 4" x 9" loaf pan.

BAKE at 325° until golden, about 70 minutes.

COOL for 10 minutes.

REMOVE from pan onto a wire rack.

*I think one could substitute any sweet dessert wine
if you couldn't find Marsala.

The slices are good toasted.

Montana State University has developed barley without a hull. The whole protein-rich grain can be eaten
just as it is grown. If you can tolerate it, you may

want to experiment with the cracked barley or bar-
ley flakes and with barley flour which makes a great
muffin. If gluten is a problem, you will want to avoid
barley.

ALL BARLEY MUFFIN

2 cups barley flour   2 tbl cooking oil
1 tbl baking powder   1 cup water
1 tsp salt   2 eggs
2 tbl sugar

PREHEAT oven to 425°.

MIX flour, baking powder, salt, and sugar together
    well.

BEAT oil, water, and eggs until blended.

ADD to dry ingredients.

STIR only until dry ingredients are moistened.

SPOON batter into greased muffin tins.

BAKE at 425° for 15 minutes or until browned.

OPTION: 1/2 cup raisins tastes wonderful.

Yields about 1 dozen muffins

Bud and Jean Clem of Western Trails, Inc. of
Bozeman, Montana, 59715 contributed this information and the tasty muffin recipe.

Teff is a special grass grown as a cereal grain in Ethiopia where it has been grown for 4,000 years. Its iron content is almost 3 times higher than wheat. Now, since 1985, it is commercially grown in Idaho. If you have a problem with gluten, you may have to avoid this.

Teff tastes a little like buckwheat. Nuts complement the taste.

TEFF MUFFINS

3/4 cup teff flour
3/4 cup rice flour
1/2 cup arrowroot*
1 1/2 tsp baking powder
1/2 tsp ground cinnamon
1/4 tsp salt

2 eggs
1/3 cup olive oil
2/3 cup water
1/2 cup chopped
    filberts

COMBINE flours, arrowroot, baking powder, spice
        and salt.

MIX eggs, oil, and water and add to the flour mixture
        mixing quickly.

POUR into greased muffin tin filling 3/4 full. (makes
        8)

BAKE in 400° oven for 25 minutes.

*May substitute potato starch or tapioca flour for arrowroot.

Kathy Forsyth of Mt Lebanon, Pennsylvania shares this recipe with us.

CINNAMON RAISIN MUFFINS

4 cups medium rye flour
1/2 cup sugar
8 tsp baking powder
1 tsp salt

2 cups dark seedless
     raisins
2 tsp ground cinnamon
8 tbl corn oil*
2 cups water

PREHEAT oven to 375°.

GREASE muffin pans.

MIX first 6 ingredients in medium bowl.

ADD corn oil and water, stirring until just moistened.

SPOON batter into muffin cups.

BAKE 30-35 minutes until muffins come away from
     edge of pan.

OPTIONAL: You can use any cooking oil or even substitute applesauce for the oil.

These muffins are my favorite!

APPLE OATMEAL MUFFINS

1 egg	1 cup quick oats
3⁄4 cup water	1⁄3 cup sugar
1 cup raisins	5 tsp baking powder
1 chopped apple	1 tsp salt
1⁄2 cup oil	1 tsp nutmeg
7⁄8 cup rice flour	2 tsp cinnamon

BEAT egg.

STIR in remaining ingredients, mixing just to moisten.

POUR into 10-12 greased muffin cups until almost
     full.

BAKE at 375° for 25-30 minutes.

Delicious hot or cold.

Very moist and flavorful!

CARROT BRAN MUFFINS

1 cup rice flour	4 eggs
1 1⁄2 cup millet or bean flour	1 1⁄2 cups vegetable oil
1 1⁄2 tbl baking powder	1 1⁄4 cups dark brown sugar
1⁄2 tsp salt	1⁄4 cup molasses
1 tbl cinnamon	3cups finely grated carrots
2 tsp Xanthan gum	1 cup raisins
2 cups bran	

COMBINE first 6 ingredients.

ADD bran and set aside.

COMBINE in a separate bowl, the beaten eggs, oil, sugar, and molasses.

ADD the carrots, raisins, and flour mixture.

FILL muffin tins nearly full.

BAKE at 325° for 30 minutes.

MAKES about 20 muffins.

Mary Jane Stoneburg came up to me in the Walnut Acres store in Penn's Creek, Pennsylvania, and handed me two of these beautiful orange muffins that she had baked specially for me! Hope you will be as impressed as I was .

MJ'S ORANGE MUFFINS

1/4 cup oil   1/2 cup rice flour
1/2 cup sugar   3 tsp baking powder
2 eggs   1/2 tsp salt
1/4 cup orange juice concentrate
1 cup water
1 1/2 cup rice flour

COMBINE the first 6 ingredients in a processor or
          by stirring well.

MIX the 1/2 cup rice flour, baking powder, and salt
          in a separate bowl.

ADD to the egg mixture and ...

POUR immediately into oiled muffin tins.

BAKE at 350° for 15-20 minutes.

Mary Jane cannot use baking powder and so substitutes 1 1/2 tsp cream of tartar and 1 tsp baking soda for the baking powder. Either way they come out very well.

She sometimes adds **one** of the following to the liquid...

> 1 cup blueberries
> 1 cup applesauce and 1⁄4 cup currants
> 2 ripe bananas
> 1 - 2 cup grated zucchini (subtract orange juice)
> 1 8 oz can crushed pineapple plus the juice (which replaces 1⁄3 of your water.)

If you really like MJ's muffins, you might appreciate the convenience of a muffin mix.

MUFFIN MIX

8 cups rice flour   2 cups sugar
4 tbl baking powder   2 tsp salt

COMBINE all ingredients.

STORE in an airtight container, preferably in the refrigerator or freezer.

TO MAKE A BATCH...

1/4 cup oil   2 1/2 cup muffin mix
2 eggs
1/4 cup orange juice concentrate
1 cup water

MIX the first 4 ingredients.

ADD the muffin mix, and stir well.

POUR immediately into greased muffin tins.

BAKE at 350° for 15-20 minutes.

You might consider adding 2 tsp ground cardamom
                or   1/2 tsp anise seeds
                or   2 tbl cocoa and 2 tsp instant
                                coffee

See pg. 53 for optional ingredients to add to your
muffins.

Using the mix...

POPPY SEED MUFFINS

1/4 cup oil   2 1/2 cup muffin
2 eggs   mix (pg.53)
1/4 cup orange juice concentrate 1/4 tsp ground
1/2 tsp grated orange peel   nutmeg

1 cup water   1/2 cup golden raisins
                               1/2 cup chopped pecans
                               6 tbl poppy seeds

MIX the first 5 ingredients.

ADD muffin mix and stir.

ADD rest of the ingredients and stir quickly until well
     mixed.

POUR immediately into greased muffin tins.

BAKE at 350° for 20-25 minutes.

From the mix...this really tastes like a bran muffin!

OAT-BRAN MUFFINS

1 cup rolled or quick oats   2 cups muffin mix
1 cup boiling water   2 cups oat bran
2 eggs, beaten   1 tsp ground cinnamon
1 1/2 cup water or fruit juice 1 cup raisins
1/2 cup molasses
1/2 cup cooking oil

PREHEAT oven to 325° F.

MIX oats with 1 cup boiling water and set aside to cool slightly.

MIX together eggs, water or juice, molasses, and oil.

ADD the oatmeal mixture and combine thoroughly.

MIX in another bowl, the mix, bran, and cinnamon.

STIR in raisins.

COMBINE the dry mixture into the liquid.

SPOON the mixture into greased muffin tins.

BAKE for 30 minutes.

Makes about 20 muffins.

If you have none of the mix, here's a recipe for 1 batch.

OAT-BRAN MUFFINS

1 cup rolled or quick oats	3⁄4 cup rice flour
1 cup boiling water	3⁄4 cup bean flour
2 eggs, beaten	1 tsp Xanthan gum

1 1/2 cup water or fruit juice 1/2 cup brown sugar
1/2 cup molasses   2 tsp baking soda
1/2 cup cooking oil   1 tsp ground
2 cups oat bran   cinnamon
                                1/2 tsp salt
                                1 cup raisins

PREHEAT oven to 325° F.

MIX oats with 1 cup boiling water and set aside to
    cool slightly.

MIX together eggs, water or juice, molasses, and
    oil.

ADD the oatmeal mixture and mix thoroughly.

MIX in another bowl, the bran, flour, sugar, soda,
    cinnamon and salt.

STIR in raisins.

COMBINE the dry mixture into the liquid.

SPOON the mixture into greased muffin tins.

BAKE for 30 minutes.

Makes about 18 muffins.

This mix makes a very light, crisp waffle or pancake.

PANCAKE MIX

2 1/2 cups rice flour   1 tbl salt
2 1/2 cups bean flour   2 tsp cream of tartar
2 1/2 cups tapioca flour   1 tsp baking soda
5 tbl baking powder   2 1/4 cups shortening
4 tsp Xanthan gum

MIX first 8 ingredients well.

ADD shortening and mix well.

STORE in sealed container in refrigerator

PANCAKES

2 1⁄4 cups Pancake Mix (Pg 58) 1 egg, beaten
1 tbl sugar (helps browning)   1-1 1⁄2 cups milk
                                              or water

COMBINE Pancake Mix and sugar.

ADD egg and milk or water, and mix well.

COOK on hot, oiled griddle for 3-4 minutes until
       browned on both sides.

makes 10-12 cakes

WAFFLES

Same recipe can be poured into preheated waffle
iron and baked until brown. Makes about 3 waffles.

This mix makes so many good things and saves so much time.

BISCUIT MIX

3 1/2 cups rice flour	1 tbl salt
3 1/2 cups bean flour	2 tsp cream of tartar
5 tbl baking powder	1 tsp baking soda
4 tsp Xanthan gum	2 1/4 cups shortening

MIX first 7 ingredients well.

ADD shortening and mix well.

STORE in sealed container in refrigerator or on a
     shelf for no longer than a month.

                    or

Substitute   3 1/2 cups rice flour
              1 3/4 cups potato starch ⟩ for the flours
              1 3/4 cups tapioca flour /   above
                    or
              3 1/2 cups rice flour
              3 1/2 cups millet flour*

This mix makes wonderful Impossible Pies, pancakes, waffles, dumplings, and coffee cake. More
recipes can be found in *Going Against the Grain
Wheat-Free Cookery.*

*If you must avoid gluten, avoid millet.

BISCUITS

3 cups Biscuit mix
2/3 - 1 cup water or milk

PREHEAT oven to 350°.

COMBINE and let stand 5 minutes.

KNEAD dough about 15 times adding flour if sticky.

ROLL out to 3⁄4" thickness.

CUT with floured biscuit cutter.

PLACE about 1" apart on unbuttered baking sheet.

BAKE 25 minutes at 350°.

You may also want to save time by spooning the dough into an 8" round cake pan, and baking for about 45 minutes.

Wonderful flavor and texture.

CHEESE BISCUITS

2 cups Biscuit Mix	1/2 cup grated Cheddar
1/4 tsp dry mustard	cheese
1/4 tsp Paprika	2/3 cup milk or water

KNEAD 5 times.

PRESS into a 8" round cake pan.

CUT dough into 8 pie shaped wedges.

BAKE in 375° oven for 35-40 minutes.

If you prefer not to use hydrogenated shortenings such as Crisco or margarine, this recipe provides the convenience of a mix, but lets you add the shortening, such as oil, later.

Mixing instructions will be different.

BISCUIT MIX TWO - WITHOUT SHORTENING

3 1/2 cups rice flour	1 tbl salt
3 1/2 cups bean flour	2 tsp cream of tartar
5 tbl baking powder	1 tsp baking soda
4 tsp Xanthan gum	

MIX first 7 ingredients well.

STORE in sealed container in refrigerator or on a shelf for several months.

If you cannot tolerate bean flour or if you need to rotate the use of flours, you may

Substitute   3 1/2 cups rice flour
              1 3/4 cups potato starch   for the flours
              1 3/4 cups tapioca flour   above
                        or
              3 1/2 cups rice flour
              3 1/2 cups millet flour*

This mix makes wonderful Impossible Pies, pancakes, waffles, dumplings, and coffee cake.

*If you must avoid gluten, avoid millet.

Recipes for BISCUIT MIX TWO allow you to add the shortening to the mix. These following recipes are for BISCUIT MIX TWO.

BISCUITS TWO

2 1⁄2 cups mix   2/3-1 cup water or milk
1⁄2 cup shortening or
    1⁄3 cup oil

PREHEAT oven to 350°.

MIX and KNEAD 10 times on lightly floured board.

ROLL out to 3⁄4" thickness.

CUT with floured cutter.

BAKE for 25 minutes or until browned.

Use only with BISCUIT MIX TWO.

PANCAKES TWO

1 egg   1 1⁄2 cups BISCUIT MIX TWO
2 tbl sugar   2 cups water
1⁄4 cup oil

MIX first 3 ingredients.

ADD mix and enough of the water to make a good
        batter.

COOK on hot, oiled griddle for 3-4 minutes until
        browned on both sides.

Makes 18 pancakes.

WAFFLES - Same recipe can be used.

This recipe is to be used with BISCUIT MIX TWO.

SHORTCAKE TWO

2 1/2 cups BISCUIT MIX TWO   1/2 cup water or
2 tbl sugar   milk
1/2 cup butter or 1/4 cup oil   1 egg, beaten
                                              Fruit, whipped
                                                  topping

PREHEAT oven to 375°.

COMBINE mix and sugar in bowl.

COMBINE melted butter or oil, water, and egg.

ADD to dry ingredients until just moistened.

KNEAD 10 times on lightly floured board.

ROLL out to 3⁄4" thickness.

CUT with floured cutter and bake about 20 minutes
        until brown.

ADD your favorite fruit and topping.

*This is based on a very old Pennsylvania Dutch
recipe. It gives you a good idea just what mashed
potatoes can do for your bread-type recipes.*

RAISED SWEET BUNS

1 cup mashed potatoes	2 tsp yeast
1 cup sugar	1 3⁄4 cups rice flour
1⁄4 tsp salt	1 3⁄4 cups millet or bean
1 1⁄4 cups water (include	flour
the potato water)	1⁄2 cup arrowroot or
1⁄4 cup lard or	tapioca
1⁄3 cup margarine	4 tsp Xanthan gum

COMBINE potatoes, sugar, salt, and lard.

DISSOLVE the yeast in the water.

ADD to potato mixture.

COMBINE the flours and Xanthan gum and add to
the potato mixture.

KNEAD the dough on a floured board adding more
flour if dough is still sticky.

PLACE in well-greased bowl and cover.

LET RISE until about double its bulk. (Overnight is
fine.)

WHEN risen, place back on floured board and pat
down to 1 inch in thickness.

CUT into "1 inch rounds" the old recipe says, but a
regular biscuit cutter is fine also.

LET rise for about 40 minutes or until dough measures about 1 1/2" in height.

SPRINKLE the tops with granulated sugar.

PLACE on well-greased baking sheet.

BAKE at 325° for about 30 minutes or until browned.

Several other countries offer delicious recipes for getting along without the use of wheat.

NORWEGIAN LEFSE

2 cups hot mashed potatoes	1 tsp salt
2 tbl butter or margarine	1 cup rice flour
1 tbl water or rice milk	1 tsp Xanthan gum

BEAT together the first 4 ingredients.

COVER and CHILL for a couple of hours.

TURN out on a lightly floured surface.

SPRINKLE the potato mixture with half of the rice
      flour.
KNEAD for 8 - 10 minutes, gradually adding the rest
      of the flour.
DIVIDE dough into small portions about the size of
      golf balls.

ROLL out to about a 6" - 8" circle.

ROLL around the rolling pin and transfer to a hot
      greased skillet or griddle.
COOK until lightly browned, 4 - 6 minutes turning
      once.

Butter and sprinkle with sugar and cinnamon and
roll lefse up to eat as bread, or wrap around a piece
of food.

NOODLES

1 3/4 cups rice flour	4 whole eggs
1 3/4 cups bean flour	5 egg yolks
3 tsp Xanthan gum	1 tbl salt

or substitute

2 1/2 cup rice flour
2/3 cup potato starch
1/3 cup tapioca flour
3 tsp Xanthan gum

ADD enough water, 1 tsp at a time, to mix dough
into a ball.

COVER with tea towel and let rest for 45 minutes.

ROLL out <u>very</u> thin. Let rest for 20-30 minutes.

CUT into noodles by rolling up and slicing with a
sharp knife or use a pasta or pizza cutter.

COOK in boiling water for 12-15 minutes.

DRAIN and add butter or 1 tbl of olive oil.

A pasta machine is a luxury, but gives a uniform thickness and size to noodles, spaghetti or macaroni.

Also good fried in vegetable oil.

RICE NOODLES

As a substitute for the wheat in pasta dishes, you might want to try rice noodles from your oriental grocer. They are very convenient.

SOAK rice noodles in warm water for 15 minutes, or until tender but firm.

DRAIN and cook in boiling water for 1 minute.

DRAIN and rinse thoroughly with cold water.

PLACE in a serving bowl.

You can add tiny shrimp, diced cucumber, sliced scallions and chopped roasted nuts for a lovely salad.

ADD an oil and wine or rice vinegar salad dressing and sprinkle with mint.

Now these really taste like pretzels...

RYE PRETZELS

1 tbl dry yeast	1 tsp salt
1 1⁄2 cups warm water	4 - 4 1⁄2 cups rye flour
1 tbl molasses	1 tbl caraway or sesame seeds
	coarse salt

DISSOLVE yeast in the warm water.

ADD molasses and salt.

STIR in flour and seeds.

KNEAD for about 5 minutes.

CUT into 12 portions.

ROLL each portion into a rope until it is about 15
     inches long.

SHAPE into pretzels or any design you wish.

PLACE on a greased baking sheet.

DAB a moistened cloth lightly on each pretzel.

SPRINKLE with a little coarse salt.

BAKE in a 425° oven for 20 minutes or until browned.

12 pretzels

SUNFLOWER CRACKERS

You may want to triple this recipe!

1 cup ground sunflower seeds
1/4 cup cold water

1/2 cup shredded
    coconut
1 tsp Xanthan
    gum or pectin

COMBINE ingredients and pat out dough on greased
    baking sheet.

PLACE a sheet of waxed paper on top of the dough.

ROLL out to the edges of the sheet with a rolling pin
    to no less than 1/8 inch.

SCORE with a knife in whatever shapes you like.

PLACE in a cold oven.

TURN oven to 300° and bake for 15-20 minutes or
    until ightly browned.

LET cool for 5 minutes before removing crackers
    from sheet.

You may wish to sprinkle some seasoning or salt on
your crackers.

HINT: The processor grinds the seeds quite well.

CAKES

MOM'S ADVICE TO HER CHILDREN
AT CHRISTMAS

1. Make a schedule to do some little thing everyday to brighten up someone's day.
   Spend some time with an older person you know.
   (Grandparent, neighbor, teacher, etc.)
2. Take a walk alone through a special garden.
   Rose Garden   Bishops's Close
   Japanese Garden   Tryon State Park
3. Take someone with you on this walk.
4. Go to watch the Christmas Parade.
5. Visit an historical house - decorated for Christmas.
6. Volunteer to serve at any of the kitchens serving the poor.
7. Play chess (checkers, Uno, Scrabble, etc.) with someone.
8. Go Christmas Caroling with friends.
9. Invite some friends over for a night of games and popcorn.
10. Clean up the kitchen for Mom so she can put up her feet!.
11. Investigate some aspect of your ancestral heritage.
    Talk or write to a relative asking about what Chistmas used to be like.
12. Don't ask for unlikely favors from your parents on your first days together.
    This insures confrontation, disappointment and guilt for everyone.
13. Help Dad with a chore.
14. Give the people around you some space. Don't make them feel badly if they aren't on your wave length.
15. Ask some older person whom you respect, what his philosophy for a good life is.
16. The more you give in terms of time the more you will receive...the more Christmas will mean to you.

"Sing a new song!!!"

December 1988

This delightful old recipe reminds me of a pound cake, but it is made with cornstarch instead of flour.

SAND CAKE

1 cup butter or margarine	5 eggs
1 tsp salt	1 1/2 cups corn
1 cup sugar	starch
	1 tsp lemon
	extract

PREHEAT oven to 350°.

COMBINE butter and salt until creamy.

ADD sugar 1 tablespoon at a time, mixing well.

SEPARATE the eggs adding 1 yolk at a time to the butter mixture.

BEAT after each addition.

RESERVE egg whites.

ADD the cornstarch 1 tablespoon at a time to the butter mixture.

STIR in lemon extract.

BEAT egg whites until soft peaks form.

FOLD gently into the batter.

GREASE and line a 9"x9" cake pan with greased
    paper

BAKE until light brown-about 40 minutes.

TEST with a toothpick. If it comes out clean, cake is
    done.

Good with fruit toppings, frosted, or just plain.

JAM CAKE

1⁄2 cup butter or cooking oil	1⁄2 tsp cloves
1 cup sugar	1⁄2 tsp nutmeg
2 eggs	1⁄2 tsp allspice
3⁄4 cup rice flour	1⁄2 cup buttermilk
3⁄4 cup bean flour	1⁄2 cup jam
1 1⁄2 tsp Xanthan gum	1⁄2 cup nutmeats
1⁄2 tsp soda	1⁄2 cup sliced
1⁄2 tsp cinnamon	citron

CREAM shortening and sugar.

ADD beaten eggs.

COMBINE flour, gum, soda, and spices.

ADD egg mixture and buttermilk to the flour.

FOLD in jam, nuts, and citron.

POUR into 8" square baking pan.

BAKE 45 minutes in a moderate oven, 350°.

Serves 12

PASSOVER SPONGE CAKE

12 eggs, separated
Pinch salt
1 1/2 cups granulated sugar

2 tbl lemon juice
1 cup plus 1 tbl
   potato starch

PREHEAT oven to 325°.

BEAT egg whites until stiff.

ADD salt.

ADD sugar slowly still beating.

COMBINE in another bowl, yolks, lemon juice, and
     potato starch.

FOLD yolk mixture gently into the egg whites.

LINE bottom of an angel-food cake pan with brown
    paper.

POUR batter into pan.

BAKE for 1 hour and 10 minutes at 325°.

DO NOT OPEN oven door while baking.

COOL cake upside down on rack.

UNMOLD by using a long serrated knife between
    cake and pan.

SERVE with fresh strawberries or fruit of your choice.

*Ann Wilkerson, from Bloomington, Indiana, sent me
this favorite cake recipe. I tried it and agree. Thank
you, Ann!*

APPLESAUCE RAISIN CAKE

2 cups ground oats   1/4 cup oil
2/3 cup sugar   2 eggs
1/2 tsp salt   1 tsp vanilla
2 tsp cinnamon   1 cup applesauce
1/2 tsp nutmeg   1 cup raisins
1 tsp soda

COMBINE ground oats, (you can grind them in your
food processor) sugar, salt, soda, and
spices in a mixing bowl.

ADD oil, eggs, and vanilla.

BEAT until smooth, about two minutes.

STIR in applesauce and raisins.

POUR batter into greased 8" square baking pan.

BAKE in preheated moderate oven (350°) 35 to 40
minutes.

COOL, cover, and store one day before serving.

(I couldn't wait that long and so tasted the cake when
still warm...very nice!)

Ann uses a burnt sugar icing on this cake, but I like
it just plain..

If you must avoid eggs, try this.

CIDER CAKE

2 cups sugar	1 tsp cinnamon
1⁄2 cup butter	1 tsp cloves or allspice
1 1⁄2 tsp baking soda	3 tsp Xanthan gum
1 1⁄2 cups rice flour	1 1⁄2 cup cider
1 1⁄2 cups bean flour	3 1⁄2 cups chopped
1⁄2 cup arrowroot or tapioca flour	raisins

CREAM butter and sugar.

COMBINE flours, baking soda and spices.

ADD to butter mixture alternately with cider, beating
well.

ADD raisins.

POUR into a greased bundt or ring-type pan.

BAKE in at 325° for about 1 1⁄2 hours.

PRUNE FLAN

1 lb prunes, pitted	3 tbl brandy
5 tbl sugar	3 large eggs
4 tbl oat or rice flour	2 cups milk or water

SOAK prunes in brandy for a day or two or more!

PREHEAT oven to 375°.

BUTTER and flour 10" baking dish with straight sides.

ADD 1 tbl sugar to prunes and combine.

LAYER prunes in baking dish.

MIX eggs in bowl with 3 tbl sugar and beat until
    blended.

COMBINE with flour and add the milk or water.

POUR mixture over the prunes.

BAKE for 45 minutes.

REMOVE flan from the oven when brown and
    bubbling.

SPRINKLE with remaining tablespoon of sugar.

COOL and serve at room temperature.

STRAWBERRY TOFU TORTE

1 1/2 cups quick or old fashioned oats
1/2 cup finely chopped almonds
1/3 cup packed brown sugar
1/3 cup margarine, melted

1 14 oz block firm or medium tofu 2 tbl lemon juice
3 eggs   1 ripe banana
2/3 cup sugar   8 oz crushed
2 tsp grated orange peel   strawberries

GREASE bottom and sides of a 10" pie or cheese
    cake pan.

COMBINE first 4 ingredients and mix well.

PRESS firmly to the bottom and sides of the pan.

PROCESS tofu, lightly, in a food processor.

ADD eggs, sugar, peel, lemon juice, and process.

ADD bananas in chunks and process until smooth.

STIR in drained, crushed strawberries.

POUR into prepared crust.

BAKE at 350° for 45-50 minutes or until firm.

COOL and top with whipped topping or crushed fruit.

OPTION - May substitute blueberries or other favorite fruit for strawberries. Leave out orange peel if adding cherries.

A blue ribbon winner, this cake took "Best of Show" at the Clackamas County Fair in 1993!

FUDGE TORTE

3⁄4 cup butter or margarine	2 tbl rice flour
6 tbl cocoa	3 eggs, separated
1 cup sugar	2 tbl water
2⁄3 cup ground blanched almonds	Chocolate glaze (pg. 85)

MELT butter in saucepan over low heat.

STIR in cocoa and 3⁄4 cup of the sugar and blend until smooth.

REMOVE from heat and cool for 5 minutes.

ADD almonds and flour.

BEAT in egg yolks, one at a time.

ADD water.

BEAT egg whites in a separate bowl until foamy.

ADD remaining sugar slowly, beating until soft peaks form.

FOLD gently the chocolate mixture into the egg whites.

POUR into greased and floured 9 inch pan.

BAKE at 350° for 30 minutes or until tester comes out clean.

COOL for 10 minutes. (Cake will settle slightly.)

REMOVE cake from pan onto rack and cool completely.

INVERT cake onto serving plate.

SPREAD with a thin coat of icing; then, let dry.

SPREAD with Chocolate Glaze and decorate if you desire.

8 to 10 servings

CHOCOLATE GLAZE

2 tbl butter or margarine	1/2 tsp vanilla
2 tbl cocoa	1 cup powdered sugar
2 tbl water	

MELT butter or margarine in small saucepan over low heat.

ADD cocoa and water.

STIR constantly until thickened; do not boil.

REMOVE from heat and add vanilla.

ADD the sugar gradually, beating until smooth.

A visit to Mary Witt down the road netted me this opinion on which version of this torte to include. "Put both of them in," she said! Tortes require very little flour and are easy to make.

THE DAIRY TORTE

1 cup dairy sour cream	3/4 cup rice flour
1 cup granulated sugar	1/2 tsp Xanthan gum
2 egg yolks	1 tbl butter or margarine, melted
1/4 tsp salt	
1/4 tsp baking soda	10 walnuts, chopped

PREHEAT oven to 300°.

GREASE an 8" or 9" cast-iron frying pan.

CUT a circle of wax or parchment paper to fit bottom.

GREASE and flour the paper.

MIX first 3 ingredients together.

MIX dry ingredients together in a separate bowl.

ADD dry ingredients to the cream mixture.

ADD butter and nuts, and mix well.

POUR into prepared pan and bake about 20 minutes or until a knife comes out clean.

COOL on a rack for 20 minutes, then turn upside down to remove cake.

REMOVE paper liner when cool enough to handle.

Mary actually chose this cake as her favorite, without knowing it was dairy-free.

THE NON-DAIRY TORTE

You may substitute 8 oz tofu for the sour cream.

BLEND the tofu in your processor or blender.

ADD 1 teaspoon vanilla or almond extract if you leave out the dairy products.

This wonderful fruit-filled pancake is a traditional French dessert from Limousin. Best when served warm.

CHERRY CLAFOUTIS

3 cups pitted sweet cherries
    soaked in 1/4 cup brandy
1/4 cup plus 1 tbl rice flour
1/4 cup plus 1 tbl bean flour
1/2 tsp Xanthan gum
1 cup sugar
Pinch salt
4 eggs

3 1/2 tbl unsalted
    butter or margarine, melted
3/4 cup water or
    cherry juice
1 1/2 tsp vanilla
    extract
confectioners'
    sugar as needed
creme fraiche or
non-dairy whipped topping

PREHEAT oven to 325°.

SOAK cherries in brandy for at least 1 hour.

BUTTER a 10" pie plate.

COMBINE flours, gum, sugar, and salt in mixing
    bowl.

ADD eggs one at a time mixing gently with a fork.

DRAIN cherries and combine juice with water to
    make 3/4 cup.

PLACE cherries in bottom of pie plate.

STIR butter and liquid into batter.

POUR batter over the cherries.

BAKE in oven for 35 minutes or until golden and set
    in the center.

COOL briefly, sprinkle with confectioners' sugar and
    serve warm with cream.

CREME FRAICHE

SHAKE 2 tbl buttermilk with 1 cup heavy cream.

LET stand in warm place until thickened 12-14 hours.

I found this recipe with some old cookbooks in a house on Whidbey Island, Washington, where we spent Christmas, 1992. I adapted it to be wheat-free.

TOPSEY TURVEY PUDDING

1/2 cup rice flour	1/4 cup shortening*
1/2 cup bean flour	2/3 cup water
1 tsp Xanthan gum	1 2/3 to 2 cups dark
2 tsp baking powder	cherries, pitted
1/4 tsp salt	1 cup cherry juice
1/2 cup sugar	1/2 cup sugar

SIFT the first 6 ingredients together.

ADD oil or softened shortening and water.

BEAT until smooth.

POUR into well-greased casserole or 8" baking dish.

PUT cherries on top.

COMBINE juice and sugar and pour over cherries.

BAKE 350° for 45 minutes.

*You can SUBSTITUTE 1/8 cup oil for the shorten-
ing. The cake will be a bit denser than if you use
shortening.

Wheat-free steamed puddings turn out so well!

STEAMED WHISKEY* PUDDING

3 tbl soft butter	1 tsp vanilla
1⁄2 cup almonds, chopped	1 tsp baking soda
1 cup pitted dates or	mixed with
3⁄4 cup raisins	2 tbl hot water
2 medium carrots, grated	1⁄2 cup rice flour
1 large potato, grated	1⁄3 cup bean flour
2 eggs	1 tsp Xanthan gum
1⁄4 tsp salt	1 tsp cinnamon
1 cup brown sugar	1⁄2 tsp ground cloves

MELT butter, grease mold and set rest aside.

CUT dates in half lengthwise.

GRATE carrots and potato by hand or in a processor.

COMBINE dates, nuts, carrots, and potato.

COMBINE eggs, salt, sugar, vanilla, and soda dissolved in hot water.

ADD to date and nut mixture.

COMBINE flours, gum, and spices.

ADD all ingredients together and stir well.

TURN batter into greased mold.

POUR rest of melted butter over the top of pudding.

COVER with lid or double thickness of foil tied on securely.

SET on a rack or jar rings in a deep kettle or canner with a lid.

ADD boiling water to canner until it reaches halfway up sides of the mold.

COVER and steam for 2 1/2 hours, keeping water boiling gently.

COOL the pudding about 10 minutes.

REMOVE from the mold.

SERVE with hard sauce flavored with brandy or cognac or any sweet fruity sauce. (See page196 &197)

*Being allergic to wheat means that you have to avoid whiskey and maybe all grain alcohol drinks, but you might be able to have brandy. If you are not sure, check with your doctor or nutritionist. This pudding doesn't really need the whiskey!!

This wonderful Christmas Plum Pudding tastes like a fruitcake.

GRANMA'S PLUM PUDDING

2 slices wheat-free
    bread, cubed
1 cup milk or water
6 oz beef suet, ground
1 cup brown sugar
2 beaten eggs
1/4 cup orange juice
1 tsp vanilla
2 cups raisins
1 cup snipped pitted dates

1/2 cup diced mixed
    candied fruits
1/2 cup chopped
    walnuts
1 cup rice flour
1 tsp Xanthan gum
2 tsp cinnamon
1 tsp ground
    cloves
1 tsp ground mace
1 tsp baking soda
1/2 tsp salt

SOAK bread in milk in a large bowl and beat to break up.

STIR in ground suet, sugar, eggs, juice, and vanilla and set aside.

COMBINE raisins, dates, candied fruits, and nuts, and set aside.

COMBINE flour, spices, soda and salt.

ADD to the fruit mixture and mix well.

STIR in the bread-suet mixture.

POUR into well-greased 2 quart mold.

COVER with a piece of tinfoil and tie with a string to secure the tinfoil.

PLACE on a rack in a large pot or canner.

ADD about an inch of boiling water.

COVER and STEAM for 4 hours.

ADD more boiling water when needed.

COOL the pudding about 10 minutes.

REMOVE from the mold.

SERVE with hard sauce or any sweet fruity sauce. (See page 95, 96, & 196)

Brought up to date for the microwave, here's a very rich raisin pudding from another old recipe.

A DICKENS OF AN ENGLISH PLUM PUDDING

2 1/2 cup raisins	1/4 tsp ground cinnamon
1/4 cup finely ground suet	1/4 tsp grated nutmeg
3 tbl fresh bread crumbs	1/4 tsp baking powder
2 tbl rice flour	1 egg beaten
3 tbl mixed glaced fruit	1/2 cup beer
2 tbl brown sugar	4 tbl brandy
1 tbl molasses	

COMBINE all ingredients except 2 tablespoons of the brandy.

GREASE a 4 cup glass or porcelain mold.

SPOON batter into the mold.

COVER with plastic wrap.

MICROWAVE on medium for 10-14 minutes or until a toothpick comes out clean.

ROTATE several times if you do not have a rotating device.

ALLOW to cool on the counter for 15 minutes.

TURN out onto a serving dish. SERVE warm or cold.

WHEN SERVING, pour remaining 2 tbl brandy into a 1 cup glass measure.

MICROWAVE on high for 15 seconds only, and pour over pudding.

LIGHT with a match.

SERVE with hard sauce or any well-flavored sauce. (See page 95, 96, & 196)

It's nearly impossible to make a real "hard" sauce without butter, so for those who can tolerate a little butter, here's a basic sauce for steamed puddings. (The British know how to warm your heart on a cold day!)

HARD SAUCE

1/3 cup butter
1 cup powdered sugar
1/2 tsp vanilla
Optional: flavor with brandy.

CREAM softened butter thoroughly.

BEAT in powdered sugar, gradually.

ADD vanilla drop by drop.

MAY add 1 tsp brandy, drop by drop.

(IF the sauce separates, add a teaspoon of boiling
        water, drop by drop.)

CHILL or serve at room temperature.

OTHER options - ADD 2 tbl strong coffee & 2 tsp
                        cocoa.
                or 2 tbl orange juice & 2 tbl grated
                        orange rind.
                or 1 tbl lemon juice & 1 tbl grated
                        lemon rind.

For your steamed puddings.

APRICOT GLAZE

2 cups apricot preserves
1 tbl brandy

WARM preserves in a saucepan over low heat until
        they melt.

STIR in the brandy.

PROCESS blender or food processor or press
    through a fine sieve.

USE a pastry brush to brush over the entire
    pudding.

This recipe will take a little time to rise...

COUNTRY FRENCH CAKE

1/2 cup milk (rice or soy)	1/4 cup sugar
1/2 cup butter or margarine	1 egg*
1 pkg active dry yeast	3 egg yolks*
1/4 cup warm water (110°)	1 1/4 cup rice flour
1/2 tsp orange peel	1 1/4 cup bean flour
1/2 tsp salt	2 tsp Xanthan gum

HEAT the milk and butter in a 1 quart pan to luke-
    warm and set aside.

MIX yeast with water and let stand 5 minutes to
    soften.

COMBINE milk mixture, grated peel, salt, sugar,
    eggs, and yeast mixture.

MIX flours and gum together and add 1 1/2 cups to
    egg mixture.

BEAT with mixer on medium or by hand for 5 min
    utes.

ADD remaining flour and beat until well blended.

DOUGH should be soft but not sticky.

TURN dough over in a greased bowl, cover and let
    rise in a warm place until doubled(about
    2 hours)

PUNCH down and turn out onto a well-greased
    12"x15" baking sheet.

FLATTEN into a greased 8" round baking
    pan.

COVER lightly with plastic wrap and let rise at room
    temperature until dough has risen to about 2
    inches. .(With heavy wheat-free dough, it may
    take an hour or two!)

BAKE in a 325° oven until a light brown, about 35
    minutes.

COOL on a wire rack.

CUT cake horizontally in half.

SPREAD filling over bottom half and replace the top
    half.

COVER lightly with plastic wrap and chill at least 6
hours.

DUST with granulated and/or powdered sugar.

Serves 12

*or a total of 4 tablespoons of egg replacer

ORANGE CUSTARD FILLING

1/3 cup sugar
1 1/2 tbl cornstarch or arrowroot*
3/4 cup light cream or rice or soy milk
2 egg yolks
1 tsp grated orange peel
1/4 cup whipping cream or use non-dairy whipped
topping

COMBINE the first 3 ingredients.

COOK over direct heat, stirring constantly until
mixture boils (about 5-7 minutes).

REMOVE from heat.

BEAT together egg yolks.

STIR in gradually, 2 tbl of the cream mixture.

STIR yolk mixture back into the cream mixture.

REMOVE from heat and stir in orange peel.

COOL, then cover and chill.

BEAT whipping cream stiffly and fold into cooled
        custard.

VARIATION: Add 2 tbl instant coffee granules with
or in place of orange peel.

* See pg. 206

This recipe came from an out of print and untrace-
able cookbook of the fifties where it was called "Old
Joe" cake! Since in the 90's that is not politically
correct, we call it

PC CHOCOLATE CAKE

1 cup brown sugar	1 tsp baking soda
1 cup granulated sugar	1 tsp vanilla
1/2 cup lard	1 1/2 cups rice
1 cup rice milk or water	flour

1/2 cup cocoa mixed with
1/2 cup boiling water

1 1/2 cups bean flour
3 tsp Xanthan gum
dash of salt

MIX sugars and lard.

ADD milk or water.

MIX cocoa and soda and add to mixture.

ADD vanilla, flours, and a pinch of salt.

BAKE at 325° for about 60 minutes.

Another old-fashioned recipe...

APPLE ROLL

apples, peeled and cored
1 cup rice flour
1 cup bean flour
2 tsp Xanthan gum
1/2 tsp salt

2 tbl sugar
4 tsp baking powder
1 tbl lard
1 egg
1/2 cup rice or soy milk

CUT apples in thin slices.

COMBINE rest of the ingredients to make the dough.

ROLL out the dough as for a pie.

COVER the dough with the apple slices.

SPRINKLE with cinnamon and roll up length wise.

CUT the roll into pieces about 2 inches long.

POUR the following syrup over the pieces.

BAKE at 350° for about half an hour.

SYRUP

2 cups granulated sugar   1 cup water

COOK the sugar in the water until it dissolves.

PIES

"Goodbye," said the fox.
"And now here is my
secret, a very simple
secret: It is only with the
heart that one can see
rightly; what is essential is
invisible to the eye.

"What is essential is
invisible to the eye," the
little prince repeated, so
that he would be sure to
remember.

Saint Exupery

A WORD ABOUT PIE CRUST...

If commercial pie makers have to adjust the flour-to-shortening ratio when the protein content of the wheat varies, I suspect that we have to constantly experiment with the ratio of rice/bean etc. flours to shortening when we make our wheat-free pie crusts. Sometimes the dough is wonderfully easy to roll out and other times, it wants to tear apart. If your dough is giving you a difficult time today, you can always press the dough into the pie pan. It is just not quite as pretty.

One can also use crusts that simply require mixing a cereal grain or nut combination and pressing this into your pie pan. An example to play with...

1 1/2 cups oats, quick or old fashioned uncooked*
1/2 cup finely chopped almonds (or filberts, pecans, cashews, etc.)
1/3 cup brown sugar
1/3 cup butter or shortening

* If you need to avoid gluten, you may use rice cereals.

COMBINE and mix well.

PRESS firmly onto bottom and sides of the pie tin.

BAKE about 18 minutes at 350°.

FOLLOW the rest of your recipe.

Write down your successes. It's all right to write in this book! Leave yourself a note for next time.

DOUBLE PIE CRUST

1 cup rice flour	1/2 tsp salt
1 cup bean flour	3/4 cup vegetable
2 tsp Xanthan gum	shortening or lard
	1/3 cup cold water

MIX with a pastry blender.

CUT in shortening and mix until particles are the size of peas.

ADD cold water and mix gently just enough to dampen entire mix.

IF mix is too sticky, sprinkle a little flour over all.

DIVIDE dough into 2 rolls.

ROLL out on lightly floured pastry cloth to desired thickness.

ROLL dough around the rolling pin to transfer to your pie pan.

FILL and cover with 2nd roll.

PRESS and flute the edges.

BAKE according to the directions in your recipe.

Out here in Oregon, the strawberry fields open about the first week in June. Pick enough for pie!

STRAWBERRY PIE

1-2 cups whole ripe strawberries
2 cups crushed strawberries
1 cup sugar
3 tbl cornstarch
1/2 tsp lemon juice
Grated lemon or orange peel

FILL a baked 9" pie crust with ripe whole berries.

BRING to a boil and simmer the crushed berries and
    sugar.

ADD cornstarch to about 1/2 cup of the strawberry
    filling and mix.

ADD this to the remaining filling.

ADD lemon juice and rind.

COOK until clear.

ADD 1 tablespoon butter to give a glazed look.

POUR over the large berries in the shell and chill.

ADD non-dairy whipped topping

AMISH PIE

1 cup dark brown sugar	1/2 cup rice flour
1/4 cup boiling water	1/2 cup bean flour
walnut-size knob of butter/margarine	
3 cups boiling water	1 tsp Xanthan gum
	1 cup granulated sugar

PUT first 3 ingredients in a pan.

STIR and boil until thick.

ADD the 3 cups of hot water.

MIX the flours, gum, and sugar with enough water
        to make a paste.

STIR this in the butter mixture.

BRING to a boil, cool, and pour in baked pie crust.

TOP with whipped topping and toasted sliced
    almonds.

Sometimes known as 'poor man's pie' here is...

AMISH SHOO-FLY PIE

3⁄4 cup rice flour	1 cup molasses
3⁄4 cup bean flour	1⁄2 cup brown sugar
1 1⁄2 tsp Xanthan gum	2 eggs
3 tbl oil	1 cup hot water
1⁄2 tsp nutmeg	1 tsp baking soda dis-
1 tsp cinnamon	solved in hot water
	2 unbaked pie crusts

MIX first 6 ingredients together until crumbly.

MIX in a separate bowl the molasses, sugar, eggs,
    water and soda.

POUR half of the syrup mixture into the unbaked pie
    crust.

ADD half of the crumb mixture.

REPEAT with the second pie crust.

BAKE at 400° for 10 minutes.

REDUCE heat to 350° for 50 minutes more.

COOL.

2 pies

Every creature on our farm appreciates, in its own way, our old King apple tree. It makes terrific cobbler.

APPLE COBBLER

1 cup cold water	1/3 cup sugar
2 tbl cornstarch	1 tsp cinnamon
2 lb. fruit or about 6 apples	1 tsp nutmeg
1/2 tsp salt	

1 recipe of shortcake batter or SWEET DOUGH
        (see pg. 120)

PEEL, core, and slice apples & place in greased
        9"x12" baking dish.

MIX water and cornstarch in saucepan.

ADD rest of ingredients.

BOIL for 5 minutes.

POUR over fruit.

POUR shortcake or SWEET DOUGH batter over
all.

BAKE at 350° for 20 minutes.

PEACH COBBLER

Substitute 2 pounds of peaches for the apples and
add 1 tsp almond extract.

*This is a fun look at how things were done in the
past. No pie plate to wash. Let us speak of...*

CABBAGES AND KINGS...AND APPLE PIES

ROLL out your pastry to about 8 inches in diameter.
　　(See page 105)

FILL one half with sliced apples.
ADD sugar or honey to taste.

SPRINKLE with about 1 tablespoon of rice flour

DOT with about 1 teaspoon of butter or margarine.

SPRINKLE with about 1/2 teaspoon of cinnamon.

MOISTEN the edges and fold empty half over the
　　apple half.

PINCH the edges together.

PLACE each of these pies on a green outer
　　cabbage leaf, flat on the bottom of the oven.

BAKE at 350° for 30 minutes.

A nicely different flavor!

Grandma Potts is very much a city lady, but I remember her picking blueberries with us out in the country...and I remember two little boys who stole the whole pie out of the freezer and ate it next door under the trees!

BLUEBERRY PIE

5 cups fresh or frozen blueberries
3 tbl rice flour
1 cup sugar or 3⁄4 cup honey
1⁄4 tsp salt
1 tbl lemon juice (omit if using wild berries)

MIX all of the ingredients gently.

MICROWAVE in a bowl for 3 minutes on "HI."

POUR mixture into a 10" pastry-lined pan.   (See
        pg.105)

DOT with 1 tablespoon of butter or margarine.

COVER with pastry top well vented.

BAKE at 350° for 40 minutes.

If you skip the MICROWAVE step, increase baking
time to 1 hour.

Even if you think you don't like rhubarb, you will want to try this delectable combination of tastes. It's good with either raspberries or strawberries.

RHUBARB RASPBERRY CUSTARD PIE

1 1/4 cups sugar
1 tbl rice flour
1/4 tsp ground nutmeg
4 beaten eggs
2 cups diced rhubarb
2 cups fresh raspberries

1/4 cup rice flour
1/4 cup sugar
1/4 cup chopped
   almonds
1/2 tsp ground cinnamon
1/2 tsp ground nutmeg
2 tbl margarine or butter

MIX first 4 ingredients in small mixing bowl and beat
    well.

COMBINE rhubarb and berries and spoon into
    uncooked 10" pastry shell.

ADD egg mixture.

CUT a square of tinfoil with a 5" hole in the center
    and cover edges of pie shell with the foil.

BAKE in 375° oven for 25 minutes.

REMOVE foil. BAKE for 15 minutes more or until
    custard is set.

COMBINE remaining ingredients.

CUT in butter with pastry cutter or fork until pieces
are the size of small peas.

REMOVE pie from oven.

SPRINKLE topping mixture around outer edge of pie
leaving a 5" circle uncovered in center.

RETURN to oven and bake 5 minutes more.

8 servings

*In the old days, this pie was a delicious example of
"making do," when fruits were expensive or hard to
come by.*

GREEN TOMATO PIE

8 medium green tomatoes	1 tbl oil
2 tbl lemon juice (or vinegar)	1 heaping tbl
1/4 tsp salt	cornstarch
1 cup sugar	1/2 cup raisins
1/4 tsp cinnamon	top and bottom
	pie crust (pg.106)

WASH tomatoes and chop or grind, removing only
stems.

PLACE in sauce pan with enough water to barely
    cover.

COOK for 15 minutes.

ADD lemon juice, salt, sugar and cinnamon.

MIX oil and cornstarch in small bowl.

ADD a tablespoon of the hot liquid.

STIR until it becomes a paste and add to sauce pan.

STIR constantly until thickened.

ADD raisins and simmer a few minutes.

LINE a 10" pie tin with crust and FILL with tomato
    mixture.

PUT top crust on, crimping edges.

BAKE at 350° for 30 minutes.

Optional: Brushing crust with egg white keeps bottom from getting soggy and makes the top crust
brown prettily.

PEACH CRUNCH

1 qt peaches (about 6 peaches)	1/2 cup sugar
1 tbl sugar	1 cup rice flour
1 tbl rice flour	2 tsp baking powder
1/2 cup peach juice or water	1/2 tsp salt
	2 tbl butter or margarine
	1 egg, beaten

PEEL and SLICE peaches into a 2 quart baking
    dish.

MIX the next 3 ingredients and pour over the
    peaches.

COMBINE the rest of the ingredients.

SPRINKLE over the peach mixture.

BAKE at 400° until browned.

This is for Little Jack Horner...

PLUM PIE

1 recipe of pastry (see page 105)	1 tsp cinnamon
2 tbl corn meal	1 cup sugar
3 cups Greengage plums	2 tsp powdered sugar

ROLL out pastry for a 9 inch pie dish.

SPRINKLE corn meal over the top.

PLACE plums in the dish.

SPRINKLE cinnamon and sugar over the top.

COVER with top crust.

BAKE at 325° for about 45 minutes.

REMOVE from oven.

SPRINKLE powdered sugar on crust.

In case I ever run into an elderberry...

ELDERBERRY PIE

2 cups ripe elderberries	juice of 1/2 lemon
3/4 cup brown sugar	1/4 tsp salt
1/4 cup rice flour	1 unbaked pastry
1/4 tsp cinnamon	shell (see page 105)

COMBINE sugar, flour, cinnamon, and salt.

ADD elderberries and lemon juice.

POUR berry mixture into unbaked pastry shell.

COVER top of pie with strips of leftover pastry or sweet dough. (See recipe for sweet dough, pg 120)

BAKE at 425° for 10 minutes.

REDUCE heat to 325° and bake for 30 more minutes.

One can reduce baking time by following the microwave instructions on page 113.

Good for the tops of elderberry pies!

SWEET DOUGH

1/2 cup rice flour	1 tsp Xanthan gum
1/2 cup bean flour	1/2 tsp baking soda
pinch of salt	1/4 cup buttermilk
1 cup brown sugar	or applesauce
	1/2 cup shortening

COMBINE dry ingredients.

ADD shortening and blend until crumbly.

DISSOLVE soda in buttermilk or applesauce and add
to dry ingredients. Add more buttermilk or
applesauce if dough is too stiff.

ROLL out on floured board and cut into strips.

PLACE on top of your pies.

This is a cookie-like crust and is best on a slightly
tart pie.

If you have any dough left, try cutting it into doughnut shapes and twisting the doughnut before baking
briefly in a medium oven.

You can garnish this delectible pie with bananas, kiwi fruit, maraschino cherries or whatever pleases you!

CHOCOLATE CREAM PIE

1 single pie crust
1 cup chocolate pudding mix
2 1/2 cups soy or rice milk
    (pg. 208)

2 tbl butter or
    margarine
1 tsp vanilla extract*
2 cups non-dairy
    whipped topping

PREPARE 9" pie crust and let cool.

COMBINE the mix and milk in a saucepan over
    medium heat.

COOK and stir until mixture thickens and bubbles.

COOK one minute longer.

REMOVE from heat and stir in butter or margarine
    and vanilla.

COOL slightly.

POUR into pie crust.

COVER with plastic wrap.

REFRIGERATE 2-3 hours.

TOP with non-dairy whipped topping, if desired.

*You can store a piece of a vanilla bean in the mix, and remove before making the pudding.

The evening library staff at Clackamas Community College snuck into the periodical storage room for some...

RAISIN PECAN PIE

2 eggs, separated	1/2 cup chopped pecans
1 cup sugar	1/2 cup raisins
1 tsp cinnamon	1 tbl melted butter
1 tsp ground cloves	1 tbl vinegar
	8" unbaked pie crust(see pg.105)

PREHEAT to 325°.

BEAT egg yolks in a medium bowl.

COMBINE sugar, cinnamon, and cloves and add to yolks.

ADD pecans, raisins, and butter.

BEAT egg whites in a separate bowl.

FOLD into the pecan mixture.

ADD vinegar.

POUR into unbaked pie crust .

BAKE at 325° until crust and top are browned, about
    30 minutes.

BE WATCHFUL, it burns easily.

COOL.

This is the real thing, just like grandma used to make.

HOMEMADE MINCEMEAT PIE

2 cups apple cider
1 cup dark brown sugar
1 1/2 lbs lean boneless
    beef chuck
1/2 lb kidney suet
1 large orange
1 large lemon
6 tart green apples

15 oz seedless raisins
    (about 2 1/2 cups)
10 oz currants
    (about 1 1/2 cups)
1/2 lb candied lemon
1/2 lb candied citron
1/2 lb candied orange
2 tsp cinnamon
1 tsp each cloves,
    allspice, & nutmeg
1 cup brandy, if desired.

COVER beef with water and simmer until tender, about 2 hours.

DRAIN and cool.

GRIND or process the beef and suet and set aside.

PEEL, core, and cut up apples and set aside.

HEAT the cider and sugar until sugar is dissolved.

STIR in the beef and suet, and mix well.

CUT the orange, lemon, and apple into quarters and remove any seeds.

PROCESS or grind until finely chopped.

COMBINE all ingredients, except for the spices and brandy, with the beef mixture.

COVER and SIMMER, stirring frequently for 1 hour.

STIR in spices and brandy and simmer, uncovered, until the liquid is reduced.

POUR into 4 one-quart jars. Seal.

STORE in the refrigerator.

ALLOW to rest for at least 3 days so that flavors mellow.

* * *

FILL a 9" pastry-lined pie dish with 3 cups
       mincemeat.

COVER with top crust, cutting slits.

BAKE at 400° for 35-40 minutes.

SERVE warm or cold.

*If sugar is a problem for you, this recipe may give
you some ideas for future pies.*

SUGAR-FREE STRAWBERRY PIE

MASH enough strawberries to fill a pie.

BRING berries to a boil.

ADD 1 package of gelatin.

COOL and then sweeten with whatever sweetener
       you can tolerate.

FILL an already baked pie shell.

COOKIES

"Food at its best is about family.
It's about how unbelievably
responsible I felt as a
little girl helping my
grandmother bake
cookies. It's about the shared
cooking and eating
memories I hope to pass along
to my kids."

--Nora Ephron, author

Ed's favorite cookies as a child. Grandma Potts made them for her children.

BUTTERSCOTCH ICE BOX COOKIES

1/2 cup butter or margarine	3/4 cup rice flour
1 cup dark brown sugar	3/4 cup bean flour
1 egg slightly beaten	1 1/2 tsp Xanthan gum
1/2 tsp vanilla	1/2 tsp cream tartar
	1/2 tsp baking soda
	1/2 cup ground nuts

CREAM butter and sugar.

ADD egg and vanilla and mix well.

MIX flours, gum, tartar, and soda and add to butter
    mixture.

ADD ground nuts.

FORM dough into a roll, wrap in waxed paper or
    plastic wrap.

REFRIGERATE for at least 2 hours.

SLICE the roll into 1/4 inch cookies.

BAKE 8 minutes at 375°, or until lightly browned.

When I first visited my mother-in-law's home, she offered me...

ALMOND CAKES

6 tbl sugar
8 oz butter or margarine
1 tsp vanilla
2 oz chopped almonds (1/2 cp)
7/8 cup rice flour
7/8 cup bean flour
2 tsp Xanthan gum

CREAM butter, sugar and vanilla.

ADD almonds, then flour.

MIX well and refrigerate for an hour.

SHAPE in 1/2 moons on greased baking sheet.

BAKE slowly at 300' for 25 minutes.

ROLL in sugar or shake in a bag of powdered
        sugar.

REMOVE from bag and cool.

                    from Grandma Irene Potts 1899 -

ANISE COOKIES

2 eggs
2/3 cup sugar
1 tsp anise seed

1 tsp Xanthan gum
1/2 cup rice flour
1/2 cup bean or millet
        flour

PREHEAT oven to 350°.

GREASE and flour a loaf pan. (approximately
    9"x5"x3")

BEAT eggs and sugar.

ADD anise seed, then the flour and Xanthan gum.

SPREAD batter in the prepared pan.

BAKE at 350° for 30 minutes. (pan will only be 1/4
    full)

REMOVE loaf from pan and slice in 1/2" slices.

PLACE slices on buttered baking sheet and bake
    for 5 minutes.

TURN and bake 5 minutes more or until sides are
    browned.

COOL. Good with fruit.

A very chewy and filling cookie with lots of good-for-you ingredients.

OAT COOKIES

3⁄4 cup sugar
1⁄3 cup margarine
1⁄3 cup honey
2 egg whites, slightly
      beaten
1 tsp almond extract

2 1⁄4 cups quick or old-
      fashioned oats,
      uncooked
1 cup oat flour
1⁄2 tsp baking soda
1⁄2 tsp salt (optional)
1⁄2 cup sliced almonds

PREHEAT oven to 350°.

BEAT sugar, margarine, and honey until fluffy.

ADD egg whites and extract.

GRADUALLY add dry ingredients mixing well.

DROP by tablespoon onto ungreased cookie sheet.

PRESS into flattened circle.

BAKE 14-16 minutes or until golden brown.

COOL for 1 minute and remove from sheet.

STORE in a tightly covered tin.

May add 1⁄3 cup raisins, chopped prunes or coconut. If you double the recipe, 3 egg whites will work.

This is an easy cookie to make - no baking! It also makes a good crumb crust for pies.

BOILED OATMEAL COOKIES

2 cup sugar	2 1/2 cup oatmeal
4 tbl cocoa	(quick cooking)
1/2 cup margarine or butter	1 tsp vanilla
1/3 cup soy or rice milk	1/3 cup peanut butter
	(optional)
	1/4 cup chopped nuts
	(optional)

MIX first 4 ingredients together in saucepan.

BRING mixture to a rolling boil for 2 minutes.

REMOVE from heat, add rest of ingredients and mix.

DROP with a spoon on waxed paper while still quite
     warm.
(Mixture becomes difficult to work with when it cools.)

MAKES 24-30 cookies.

Sometimes coconut is packaged with preservatives to sweeten it and keep it soft. If you are sensitive to such things, read the label. This recipe uses the dry coconut.*

COCONUT COOKIES

3 eggs	1 1/2 cups oat flour**
1/2 cup honey	2 tsp baking powder
2 tbl oil	1 tsp Xanthan gum
2 cups coconut shreds	candied cherries

BEAT the first 3 ingredients.

ADD coconut.

MIX flour, baking powder, and gum.

ADD to coconut mixture.

MIX thoroughly and drop small cookies on greased cookie sheet.

FLATTEN lightly and top with 1/2 candied cherry.

BAKE at 325° for 10 minutes.

*In converting your **own** recipes, when you are substituting dry coconut for the moistened, ADD 1 1/2 tsp water for each 1/2 cup of dry unsweetened coconut.

**You may substitute rice or almost any flour here.

TOFU BARS

4 tbl butter or margarine   1 tsp vanilla
1/2 cup honey   1/4 tsp salt
                              1/3 cup tofu
                              1/2 cup rice flour
                              1/2 tsp Xanthan gum
                              1 tsp baking soda
                              1 tsp baking powder
                              1/2 cup chopped nuts

PREHEAT oven to 325°.

MELT butter and stir in honey.

COMBINE the next 7 ingredients into processor or
    blender.

MIX until well blended.

SPRINKLE chopped nuts on top.

BAKE at 325° for 40 minutes.

COOL and cut into bars.

SUPERMOUSE BARS

1/4 cup honey	3/4 cup oat or rice bran
2 tbl oil	3/4 cup rolled oats
3 tbl peanut butter	1/2 cup unsweetened coconut
	1/2 cup finely chopped apricots

MELT peanut butter, honey, and oil together in large saucepan.

ADD remaining ingredients and mix well.

STIR for 5 minutes and remove from heat.

GREASE an 8" x 8" pan.

PRESS mixture evenly into the pan.

REFRIGERATE until firm and cut into bars.

PEANUT BUTTER COOKIES

1/2 cup margarine or butter	3/4 cup bean flour
1/2 cup peanut butter	1/2 cup potato starch
1 cup brown sugar, packed	1/2 tsp baking soda
1/2 tsp vanilla	1/2 tsp salt
	1 tsp Xanthan gum

BEAT shortening, peanut butter, sugar, and vanilla until creamy.

MIX flours, baking soda, salt and Xanthan gum.*

ADD to sugar mixture, beating well.

ROLL dough into 1 inch balls.

PLACE about 2 inches apart on greased baking sheet.

PRESS balls with a fork to make the crisscross pattern.

BAKE 15 minutes at 350° until slightly browned.

REMOVE cookies from pan and cool.

*You can omit the Xanthan gum if you add 1 egg.

*Nut butters can be made in your food processor.
Toasting nuts improves the flavor.*

ALMOND BUTTER COOKIES

1 cup almond butter	1 tsp almond extract
1/2 cup honey	1/4 tsp salt
1/4 cup almond oil*	2 cups arrowroot flour

optional: 1 tsp Xanthan gum

PREHEAT oven to 350°.

COMBINE butter, honey, and oil and blend until
        smooth.

ADD extract and salt.

ADD flour a little at a time and mix well.

FORM dough into balls and place on greased cookie
        sheet.

FLATTEN balls with a fork to about 1/2 inch
        thickness.

BAKE about 10 minutes.

Uncooked dough keeps well in the refrigerator.

*There is room for much substituting with this recipe.
You can experiment with different oils, nuts and
flours. Bean flour makes for a totally different texture.

If you have to avoid eggs, you'll like these very crisp cookies - great for dunking. Very crisp cookies were prized in days gone by, for their preservative qualities. They can be softened by adding a little piece of apple to the cookie tin.

GINGERSNAPS

1 cup molasses	3 tsp Xanthan gum
1/2 cup sugar	1 tsp baking soda
3 tbl butter or margarine	1 tsp cloves
3 tbl lard	1 tsp cinnamon
2 tbl water	1 tsp ginger
1 1/2 cup rice flour	1 tsp salt
1 1/2 cup bean flour	

BRING molasses to a boil in saucepan.

ADD sugar, shortening, and water.

COMBINE dry ingredients and add to sugar mixture.

CHILL overnight.

ROLL out dough to about 1/8 inch thickness.

CUT into rounds or gingerbread men.

BAKE on ungreased cookie sheet at 325° for about 10 minutes.

You can also form the dough into a log shape and then slice it into 1/8 inch slices when you take it out of the refrigerator.

about 10 dozen

Another cookie without eggs, this recipe is adapted from Pennsylvania Dutch Cookery *by Ann Hark and Preston Barba.*

HEIFER TONGUES

2 cups brown sugar
1 cup shortening
1 cup molasses
2 1/2 cup rice flour
2 cups bean flour

4 tsp Xanthan gum
1/2 cup warm water
1 tsp baking soda
1 tsp cinnamon

CREAM sugar and shortening.

ADD molasses.

DISSOLVE soda in the warm water.

COMBINE flours, gum and cinnamon.

ADD flours and water alternately to the molasses
        mixture.
MIX well and shape dough into a long roll about
        2 1/2 inches in diameter.
FLATTEN it slightly and refrigerate overnight.

CUT into 1/4" slices.

PLACE on ungreased cookie sheet

BAKE at 350° for about 12 minutes.

50 cookies

*A Pennsylvania Dutch specialty and a wonderful cookie with the added bonus of **not** needing eggs. Caroline Schnoor, of Portland, Oregon, explains that the Christmas baking used to start way before Christmas, so the cookies were very hard in order to preserve them. They would have softened by Christmas or a piece of apple would be enclosed in the cookie tin for a day or two.*

LEBKUCHEN

1 1⁄2 cups honey	1⁄2 tsp ground cloves
2 1⁄4 cups brown sugar	1⁄2 tsp mace
1⁄2 cup butter or margarine	1⁄2 tsp ground cardamom
3 cup rice flour	1⁄2 tsp salt
2 1⁄2 cup bean flour	1 tsp cinnamon
5 tsp Xanthan gum	3⁄4 cup chopped citron
	1 1⁄4 cup chopped almonds

HEAT honey, sugar, and butter or margarine.

COMBINE flours, salt, gum and spices.

ADD to honey mixture and stir.

ADD citron and nuts.

KNEAD dough and place in a covered bowl.

SET aside for a week in a cool place.

ROLL out to 1/4 inch thickness. (Takes a bit of
elbow grease to roll these!)

PLACE on greased baking sheets, or press into
cookie tin with a rim on it.

BAKE at 325° until dark brown-about 15 minutes.

REMOVE from oven and brush with glaze. (below)

CUT into squares while still warm.

These keep very well in a tightly closed cookie tin.

*My friend, Carol Groff from Canby, Oregon treats
her family to Lebkuchen with this glaze.*

LEBKUCHEN GLAZE

2 tbl water
1 cup powdered sugar
1 tsp lemon juice

MIX together and spread over your Lebkuchen.

*A Moravian Christmas (German) cake- another won-
derful eggless cookie! This cookie was also a hard
cookie for preservation purposes in the "old days!"*

LECKERLE

1 1/2 tsp baking soda	2 cups rice flour
2 cups molasses	2 cups bean flour
1/4 cup melted butter/	4 tsp Xanthan gum
margarine	1/3 cup diced citron
1 cup brown sugar	1/4 cup chopped,
1 1/2 tsp ground cloves	blanched almonds
1 tbl cinnamon	1 oz brandy (2 tbl)

ADD soda to a tablespoon warm water.

HEAT molasses and add butter, sugar, spices, nuts,
    citron, and soda.

MIX flours and gum and add to the molasses
    mixture a little at a time.

ADD brandy a little at a time.

**COVER the dough and set aside in a cool place for
    2 weeks.**

ROLL out the dough 1/4 inch thin on a lightly floured
    board. (with vigor!)

CUT into squares about 4 inches square. (You can
    cut them smaller!)

BAKE at 325° for about 15 minutes.

These cakes will keep for about 2 months in a tightly closed cookie tin.

These Pennsylvania Dutch Springerle cookies are unique in that one uses a mold pressed upon the rolled out dough.

Caroline Schnoor, of Portland, Oregon, explains that these cookies were made very hard in order to preserve them. A piece of apple would be enclosed in the cookie tin for a day or two to soften them.

SPRINGERLE

2 eggs*	3⁄4 cup rice flour
1 cup granulated sugar	3⁄4 cup bean flour
1 lemon rind, grated	1 1⁄2 tsp Xanthan gum
2 tsp aniseed or	1 tsp baking powder or
a few drops anise oil	baking soda
	1⁄4 tsp salt

BEAT eggs lightly. *(You can omit the eggs.)

ADD sugar slowly and beat for 15 minutes.

ADD grated lemon.

ADD rest of the dry ingredients. If dough is still
    rather soft, knead in a little more flour.

ROLL out to 1/4 inch thickness and as close as
    possible to the shape of your Springerle mold.

FLOUR the surface of the dough and then press the
    mold down hard on the dough.

CUT into little squares. (a pizza cutter is good for
    this)

PLACE on greased and floured cookie sheets and
    set aside overnight to dry and set the impres-
    sions on the dough.

BAKE at 300° for 25 minutes. Do not brown. These
    will be very crisp.

In the "old days", the cookies would be left on your
kitchen counter to cure. Now, we suggest if you use
eggs that you **refrigerate** the tray for 24 hours.
Cover lightly with a cloth.

How long has it been since you've had an ice cream cone?

ICE CREAM CONES

3 eggs*   1 tsp Xanthan gum
1/2 cup rice flour   1 cup sugar
1/4 cup arrowroot   1 tbl water
1/4 cup bean flour

WHIP up the eggs, flours, gum, and sugar.

ADD the tablespoon of water, more if the dough is
        too thick to spread. (It should feel like you
        are spreading bubble gum!!)

GREASE a cookie tin.

PLACE spoonfuls of batter about the size of a ping-
        pong ball on the cookie tin.

USE a spatula dipped in cold water to smooth each
        ball of dough, thinly, into an oval pancake.

BAKE at 350° until just barely browned - about 10
        minutes.

REMOVE from oven and remove each pancake,
        rolling it into a cone shape. You need to do
        this right away before the cones become too
        crisp. (I use a rubber glove on my left hand
        to keep from burning my fingers, and I use

the spatula in my right hand to loosen the pan cakes. **You** might devise a better way!!)

STORE in an air-tight tin to use later.

WARNING: These are good enough to disappear before you ever get to filling them!!

*I have done these with Ener-g Foods Egg Replacer found at your health food store. You may have to experiment a little.

MAIN COURSE

Wisdom has built her house,
*   she has set up her seven columns;*
She has dressed her meat, mixed her wine,
*   yes, she has spread her table.*
She has sent out her maidens; she calls
*   from the heights out over the city:*
"Let whoever is simple turn in here;
*   to him who lacks understanding, I say,*
Come, eat of my food,
*   and drink of the wine I have mixed!*
Forsake foolishness that you may live;
*   advance in the way of understanding."*

*   from the book of Proverbs.*

Another way to use the Biscuit Mix.

RING AROUND THE VEGIES

3 cups Biscuit mix (pg.60)
2⁄3 - 1 cup water or milk
1 pound (3or 4 small)
    red potatoes
1 1⁄2 cups cooked broccoli

2 tbl canola oil or
    butter
2 tbl bean or rice flour
1⁄2 tsp salt
2 cups rice (or soy)
    milk
1⁄3 cup shredded
    cheese*
1 tbl parsley
1 tbl basil (optional)

MIX Biscuit mix with the water.

DROP by the spoonful around the edge of a pie plate leaving center open.

BAKE for 25 minutes at 350°.

CUT potatoes in half and cook in water over medium heat until tender.

COOK broccoli in small amount of water for about 8 minutes and drain.

MIX oil, flour, salt in a saucepan or skillet to make a paste.

HEAT and ADD the rice milk and cheese.

STIR until thickened.

ADD drained potatoes and broccoli to the white
     sauce.

SPOON potato-sauce mixture into the biscuit ring
      and serve.

* Try almond or soy cheese from your healthfood
store if dairy is a problem.

You can experiment with different kinds of vegetables
and sauces. A couple tablespoons of sherry and a
little ham is also good!

As close as we can come to a real...

PIZZA CRUST

1 1/2 cup rice flour	1/2 tsp salt
1 1/2 cups bean flour	1/2 cup oil
3 tsp Xanthan gum	1 cup milk or water
3 tsp baking powder	

PREHEAT oven to 325°.

COMBINE flours, gum, salt and baking powder in
         large bowl.

ADD water or milk, and oil and mix well.

KNEAD until smooth. (10 minutes)

ROLL out onto oiled pizza or cookie trays.

BRUSH lightly around the edges with cooking oil.
(Fingers work well!)

SPREAD with a can of tomato paste or sauce.

ADD oregano and/or basil to taste.

COVER with grated mozzarella or jack cheese.*

ADD whatever suits your fancy: crumbled hamburger, sliced sausage, olives, onions, tomatoes, anchovies, mushrooms, pineapple,
shrimp (cooked).

SPRINKLE lightly with Parmesan grated cheese.

BAKE for 10 minutes at 350°, then for 10 minutes at
400°.

SERVE hot or freeze and reheat when ready.

*If dairy is a problem, you may want to try one of the
"fake" cheeses made from tofu or almond...found at
your health food store.

This is very filling and you can vary the meat portion.

HEARTY STUFFED POTATOES

2 large baking potatoes
1/2 pound pork sausage
1 medium onion, chopped
1 medium green pepper,
    sliced

1 8oz can tomato
    sauce
1/2 cup water
1/2 tsp dried oregano
    leaves
Dash hot pepper
    sauce

SCRUB each potato and prick with a fork.

BAKE in a 375° oven for 40-60 minutes or MICRO-
    WAVE on HI for 8-10 minutes rotating after 4
    minutes.

COOK pork sausage, onion and green pepper in
    large frying pan over medium-high heat for
    5-6 minutes.

POUR off drippings.

STIR in tomato sauce, water, oregano and pepper
    sauce.

COOK over low heat for 7-10 minutes, stirring occa-
    sionally.

CUT potatoes lengthwise in half and gently push
ends to open up.

SPOON the sausage mixture into each potato half
and serve.

Serves 4

*My grown children would rate their Mom a "0" if she
didn't fix this dish for the holidays!*

HOLIDAY SWEET POTATOES

3 large sweet potatoes
(or yams)
1/2 cup frozen orange juice
concentrate
2 tbl brown sugar
1/2 cup walnut or pecan
halves

1/4 cup butter or 1/8 oil
6 slices cooked bacon,
chopped
2 cups miniature
marshmallows

CUT potatoes or yams into 1/2 inch chunks.

ADD water to just cover and BOIL until easily pierced
with a fork.

PLACE vegetable into a casserole dish.

COMBINE rest of ingredients, except for marshmal
  lows, and pour over potatoes.

COVER top with the marshmallows.

BAKE at 350° for 20 minutes or until marshmallows
  are light brown.

*If you don't have any noodles, you can still have
lasagne...*

POTATO LASAGNE

1/4 cup oil	10 oz frozen chopped
1/2 cup rice flour	spinach
2 cups rice milk	5 large russet potatoes
2 cups chicken broth	(about 2 1/2 lbs)
1/4 tsp nutmeg	1 large red onion thinly
1 cup (4oz) each havarti,	sliced
provolone or Swiss	1/4 lb thinly sliced
cheeses, shredded	prosciutto or ham
(or all of one kind)	cut into slivers
pepper	

HEAT oil and flour in 2 qt. saucepan until bubbly.

REMOVE from heat and add milk, broth, and
       nutmeg.
HEAT until boiling.

REMOVE from heat and add 1 cup of grated cheese
       at a time.

STIR until smooth and add pepper to taste.

BUTTER a 9"x13" baking dish.

PEEL and slice potatoes.

ARRANGE 1/3 of potato slices in bottom of pan.

COVER with 1/2 of the onion, 1/2 of prosciutto and
       1/2 of drained spinach.

POUR 1/3 of the cheese sauce over the top.

REPEAT layering process ending with potatoes and
       cheese sauce.

BAKE covered in a 375° oven for 30 minutes.

REMOVE cover and continue baking for 1 hour.

SPRINKLE parmesan cheese over lasagne and
       bake 5 minutes longer.

LET stand 10 minutes before serving.

Serves 6

COUNTRY CABBAGE

1 large cabbage, coarsely chopped
1 medium red onion, chopped
1/2 bell pepper, chopped
1/2 lb lean ground pork
1/2 lb lean ground beef
2 or 3 fresh basil leaves (or 1 tbl dried)

1 sprig parsley (or 1 tbl dried)
1/2 tsp salt
1/8 tsp black pepper
1 quart canned tomatoes
1 cup tomato puree

BROWN ground meat and pour off all but 2 table spoons of oil.

PLACE all ingredients in large stew pot.

SIMMER until meat and vegetables are tender, about 45 minutes.

SERVE in soup bowls with your new recipe for sour-dough bread, (p. 32)

RED CABBAGE

1 medium-sized head red cabbage	2 tart apples, chopped
4 tbl butter or margarine	6 cloves
	1 glass red wine (optional)

1 medium-sized head
        red cabbage
4 tbl butter or margarine

2 tart apples, chopped
6 cloves
1 glass red wine (optional)

SLICE thinly and chop cabbage.

COMBINE cabbage, butter, apples, and cloves.

COOK for about 15 minutes until tender.

Probably a good idea to remove the cloves!

ADD wine and simmer for a minute more.

Here's something special!

CLUCKING PEAR STIR-FRY

3⁄4 cup cold water
3 tbl frozen orange juice
2 tbl tamari*
2 tsp cornstarch
1⁄4 tsp ground ginger
1⁄4 tsp ground cinnamon
dash red pepper

1⁄4 cup sliced almonds
1 tbl cooking oil
small can mushrooms
2 medium sweet
   peppers, sliced
2 medium unpeeled
   pears, sliced
12 oz skinless, boned
   chicken in 1" pieces
Hot cooked brown rice

COMBINE first seven ingredients and set aside.

PREHEAT skillet or wok over medium high heat.

STIR-FRY almonds for 1 minute to toast and remove.

STIR-FRY mushrooms, peppers and pears in the
    oil till crisp-tender and remove.

ADD chicken, cooking for 3 minutes or until tender.

PUSH chicken to the side.

ADD sauce, cooking until thickened.

STIR in chicken and pear mixture and heat.

ADD almonds and serve over rice.

*Tamari can be found in a health food or specialty store. It is wheat-free soy sauce.

serves 4

CHEESE-STUFFED SQUASH

2 or 3 large zucchini or crookneck squash
1 small onion minced
2 tbl bacon drippings or butter or oil
1/2 tsp salt
1/4 tsp pepper

1 cup fine wheat-free bread crumbs
1/2 cup sliced, cooked mushrooms
1/3 cup shredded cheddar cheese*
3 slices bacon, partially cooked

HALVE the squash and MICROWAVE until barely tender - 5 minutes per pound of squash.

COOL and CUT squash in half.

SCOOP out pulp, leaving shells about 1/4" thick.

COOK onion in butter or oil until tender but not browned.

ADD squash pulp, salt, pepper, crumbs and mushrooms.

MIX well and spoon into squash shells.

ARRANGE in shallow baking dish and top with
    cheese.

CUT bacon strips in halves and put on top of squash.

BAKE at 400° for 15 minutes or until browned.

MAKES 6 servings.

*If you cannot tolerate dairy cheese, try some
almond or soy cheese from your healthfood store.

STIR FRIED RICE

*This is a very adaptable dish. You can experiment
with many vegetables.*

1/2 onion chopped   2-3 cups cold cooked
2 stalks celery chopped   rice
1 raw egg   2 tbl tamari sauce*
                                        (wheat-free soy sauce)

SAUTE the onion and celery in a skillet.

ADD the cold rice.

ADD the raw egg and stir well.

SERVE when thoroughly hot.

Salmon tastes delicious added to the stir fry but, you may add any leftover vegetables and/or meat.

*Tamari can be found in a health food or specialty store.

FILBERT RICE

4 cups cooked Basmati or   3 tbl canola oil
        brown rice   salt to taste
1/2 cup coarsely ground filbert nuts
1/4 cup dried parsley

COMBINE all ingredients and warm for 5-10
      minutes in 300° oven.

SPRINKLE 1/3 cup grated Parmesan cheese on top.

BROIL for 3-5 minutes.

There are several ways to do...

FRIED GREEN TOMATOES

6 large green tomatoes	cornmeal, cornflour,
1 beaten egg	arrowroot* or rice flour
	bacon grease or cooking
	oil

WASH and trim off ends of tomatoes.

SLICE and dip into beaten egg.

DIP into plate of meal or flour.

FRY one side in 1⁄4 inch bacon grease or cooking
oil.

TURN over and fry on other side.

LIFT onto a platter and serve.

ANOTHER old-fashioned way to prepare fried green
tomatoes is very good, although it contains
quite a bit more fat.

POUR 3⁄4 cup heavy cream or non-dairy creamer
into the skillet after removing tomatoes.

ADD 1 tablespoon basil or parsley.

COOK slowly stirring to scrape up browned bits. DO
NOT boil.

POUR over tomatoes and serve at once.

6 servings

*arrowroot, see pg 206.

Don't throw out those green tomatoes at the end of summer. Slice them, coat them and freeze them.

FRIED GREEN TOMATOES FOR ANOTHER DAY!

SLICE tomatoes 3⁄4 inch thick.

COAT in meal or flour.

SEASON with salt, pepper and basil.

FREEZE in one layer on a cookie sheet.
　　　When frozen, transfer to containers.

PANFRY without thawing for 10 minutes, turning
　　　　　once.

There are so many good things to do with your "not so successful" experiments with bread. Save your leftovers for recipes like the following...

STEWED BREAD

1/2 onion, sliced
1/2 cup chopped green pepper or celery
1 can tomatoes
2-3 slices extraneous bread!
1 tsp basil

SAUTE onion, and pepper or celery until softened.

ADD tomatoes and basil.

CUBE the bread and add to the mixture.

HEAT thoroughly.

The aroma when this is baking is "out of this world!" Husband, Ed, tells me that kugel is usually served as a side dish with dinner, but it can also be a dessert.

APPLE KUGEL

1/2 lb wheat-free noodles (pg 69)   1/2 tsp salt
    (about 4 cups loose uncooked) 1 tsp vanilla
10 tbl unsulfured molasses   2 tsp dried basil
1/4 cup boiling water   2 large apples
4 large eggs   1 cup raisins
3 tbl oat bran (optional)   1 tsp cinnamon

COOK noodles and drain well.

COOK molasses in large skillet on low heat until
    mixture bubbles.

ADD the boiling water, remove from heat and add
    noodles.

BEAT eggs and ADD to the skillet with bran, salt,
    vanilla and basil.

PEEL and core the apples.

CHOP or put briefly into the processor.

GREASE a large casserole.

POUR mixture in and gently add apples and raisins.

SPRINKLE cinnamon on top.

BAKE at 350° for about 30 minutes or until top is
    crisp.

6-8 servings

ANTIPASTO

1 cup green (bell) pepper cut in 1 inch pieces
1 cup sliced mushrooms
1/2 cup diced Jack or Swiss cheese
1 small jar artichoke hearts
3 or 4 anchovies cut in small pieces
1 tbl dried parsley or 1/4 chopped fresh parsley
1/4 cup chopped basil
3 tbl wine or cider vinegar
1/4 cup olive oil
salt and pepper to taste

RUB a bowl with a clove of garlic.

COMBINE all ingredients.

OPTIONAL: Try 1 tbl of Dijon-style mustard. (Check the vinegar used in your mustards if you must be avoid grains.)

SOUPS

HOW WE ARE WITH WORDS IS HOW WE ARE WITH EACH OTHER... BECAUSE WORDS ARE BEINGS LIKE WE ARE BEINGS. THEY ARE MADE OF LINES AND LETTERS AND SPIRIT AND WE ARE MADE OF FLESH, BLOOD, BONES AND SPIRIT. WE CAN BE AS CLOSE WITH THEM OR FAR AWAY AS WITH EACH OTHER. WE CAN HIDE BEHIND THEM OR OFFER THEM AS GIFTS. THEY CAN CATCH US BY SURPRISE LIKE LONG-LOST FRIENDS JUMPING OUT AT US FROM FOLDS SO DEEP INSIDE OUR HEARTS THAT ANGELS ALSO COULD LIE HIDDEN THERE.

PILLOW MOUNTAIN, Notes On Inhabiting A Living Planet ©1988, 1991 by Michael Bridge; Published by TIMES CHANGE PRESS, P.O. Box 1380, Ojai, California 93024-1380

Here is a painless way to increase your calcium.

KALE SOUP

1/2 cup sauteed onions   4 cups boiling water
1 cup diced potatoes   3 tbl oil
2 cups minced kale   1 tsp salt.

COMBINE onion, potatoes, kale, salt, and water.

PUREE at least 3/4 of the soup in your processor or
    blender.

COOK 20-30 minutes.

6 servings

Option: May substitute 1 or 2 cups soy or rice milk.

MOBY DICK CHOWDER

2 cups cooked kale or spinach   1 tbl butter or
2 cups rice or soy milk   canola oil
2 cans clams*   salt & pepper
                            dash of nutmeg

DRAIN the kale or spinach.

PUT in blender or processor with the clams, including the juice.

PROCESS for 10 seconds.

POUR into a saucepan.

ADD rice milk and bring just barely to a boil.

ADD butter and seasonings.

4-6 servings

*Shrimp is also good!

A wonderful start to your meal...

CIDER SOUP

2 quarts cider   3 tbl rice or bean flour
1/2 cup sugar   allspice or nutmeg to taste
3 beaten eggs   3 cups diced wheat-free
2 cups rice or soy milk   bread*
                                butter or margarine

BOIL the cider and skim if necessary.

COMBINE the sugar, eggs and milk.

ADD the flour and spice.

*USE up some of your less successful experiments and BROWN the diced bread in a little butter.

SPRINKLE bread on top and serve.

Serves 6

GARDEN POTATO SOUP

4 medium potatoes, diced   6 cups water
4 medium tomatoes, quartered   1 tsp salt
a few sprigs of marjoram, thyme 1 tb butter
     or parsley (or 1/2 tsp of
     your choice, dried)

BOIL all ingredients, except salt and butter, until a
     smooth consistency.

ADD salt and butter and serve.

Optional: You may wish to run this cooked soup
     through your blender or processor.

A wonderful Spanish soup and so easy to make.

GAZPACHO

1 chopped cucumber	3 tbl salad oil
1/2 green pepper, chopped	2 tbl wine vinegar
1 small onion finely chopped	1 tbl dried oregano
2 tomatoes chopped	or basil
4 cups tomato juice	1/2 avocado, diced
	salt and pepper to taste

PUT aside about 1/2 cup of the chopped vegetables.

PLACE the rest of the ingredients in a blender or processor and blend or puree.

ADD the 1/2 cup of the vegetables back into the soup.

COVER and chill for at least 2 hours.

from the kitchen of Jim Knull, Grapeview, WA.

SAUCES

The fact is
that it takes more than
ingredients and technique
to cook a good meal.
A good cook puts something
of himself into the preparation--
he cooks with enjoyment,
anticipation
spontaneity,
and he is willing
to experiment.

Pearl's Kitchen,
Pearl Bailey 1973

You might assume that a sauce would be wheat-free, but one look at the label would surprise you. If you make your own, you know what's in it. You also avoid problems with preservatives. If you have to avoid distilled vinegar, you may find it easier to make your own catsup. **Jeanne Huffstutter** *of Portland, Oregon shares this very good recipe, using cider vinegar.*

JUST CATSUP

8 oz tomato sauce	1/2 stick cinnamon
6 oz tomato paste	1/8 tsp ground cloves
2 oz water	3/8 tsp paprika
1/3 cup cider vinegar	1/2 tsp dry mustard
1/4 tbl ground allspice	dash cayenne

COMBINE all ingredients in a saucepan.

SIMMER, stirring to prevent sticking, until thick - about 45 minutes.

OR , MICROWAVE on HI for 4 minutes (turn once). MICROWAVE on medium low for 10 minutes.

REMOVE cinnamon stick, and cool.

KEEP refrigerated.

Optional: You may substitute wine or rice vinegar for the cider vinegar.

Mustard is a fun food to make. It will NEVER go bad. It may dry out and lose its flavor but it will not be harmful to you. It is good for holding together the oil and vinegar in your salad dressing. Good with your grilled cheese sandwich.

SPICY MUSTARD

1/3 cup light mustard seeds
1/4 cup dry mustard
1/2 cup cold water
1 cup cider vinegar
2 tbl brown sugar
1 tsp salt
2 cloves garlic, minced

1/2 tsp ground cinnamon
1/4 tsp ground allspice
1/4 tsp dill seeds
1/4 tsp dry tarragon
1/8 tsp ground turmeric
1 - 2 tbl honey

SOAK seeds and mustard in cold water for 3 hours.

COMBINE vinegar, sugar, salt, garlic, cinnamon, all spice, dill, tarragon and turmeric in a 1 quart non-corroding pan.

SIMMER over medium heat for about 15 minutes, until liquid is reduced by half.

POUR liquid through a strainer into the mustard mixture.

PUREE in a blender or processor.

COOK in the top of a double boiler until thickened- about 10 to 15 minutes. Mixture will thicken more as it cools.

STIR in 1-2 tablespoons honey.

COOL and pack into a jar, covering tightly.

STORE in refrigerator for at least a week or up to 2
    years.

*This delightful mustard comes from mustard expert,
Helene Sawyer, of Canby, Oregon.* [1]

BASIC DIJON-STYLE MUSTARD

2 cups dry white wine   3 tbl honey
1 large onion, chopped   1 tbl oil
3 cloves garlic, pressed   2 tsp salt
1 cup (4 oz.) dry mustard

COMBINE wine, onion, and garlic in a saucepan.

HEAT to boiling and simmer 5 minutes.

COOL and discard strained solids.

ADD this liquid to dry mustard, stirring constantly
    until smooth.

BLEND in honey, oil, and salt.

RETURN to saucepan (have hankies ready or hold
    face away from steam)

HEAT slowly until thickened, stirring constantly.

COOL; place in covered jar.

AGE in cool, dark place 2 to 8 weeks, depending
    upon pungency desired.

Then REFRIGERATE.

*You can be creative here, adding honey, or herbs,
or using wine or rice or apple cider vinegar, but **not**
grain vinegar, and blending well with the basic recipe.*

1. Printed with permission from Helene Sawyer, author of *Gourmet
Mustards: How to Make and Cook with Them,* published by Culinary
Arts Ltd., Lake Oswego, Oregon, 97035.

🍓   🍓   🍓

*This is an excellent substitute for your regular spa-
ghetti sauce.*

PESTO SAUCE

1 oz piece Parmesan cheese   1 cup fresh basil
1/4 cup walnuts   leaves *
black pepper to taste   1/2 tsp salt
2-3 cloves garlic   1/3 cup olive oil

USE processor to grate cheese.

MEASURE 1/4 cup cheese into mixing bowl.

PROCESS nuts briefly to chop them and add to
cheese.

PROCESS olive oil and basil leaves until nearly
smooth.

COMBINE all ingredients.

ADD extra oil if mix is not runny.

STORE in a 1 cup jar and clean pesto from sides of
jar.

POUR a little olive oil over the top and store in your
refrigerator.

REPEAT this storing process each time you use the
pesto. Keeps about a year in your refrigerator.

Use over corn or rice pasta with fresh tomatoes,
shrimp, peas and a little lemon juice.

*(or 1 cup firmly packed parsley plus 1 tbl. dried sweet
basil)

Mixes well with tuna.

EGGFREE MAYONNAISE

1/4 cup wine or cider vinegar   1 tsp sugar or honey
3/4 cup olive oil   1 tsp Dijion mustard
1 tsp salt   1 cup mashed pota-
                 toes*
     optional: pinch of
                 herbs

COMBINE first 5 ingredients.

PROCESS in a blender or food processor.

ADD enough potatoes, preferably hot, to thicken.

ADD choice of your favorite herbs. (Parsley, dill, or basil are good.)

THICKENS as it cools.

REFRIGERATE in a **labelled** jar.

*You may want to try substituting 1 cup tofu for the 1 cup of potatoes.

Wonderful with fish, especially catfish!

PECAN BUTTER SAUCE

1/2 cup finely chopped pecans
1/4 cup butter or margarine
1 tbl lemon juice
1 tsp Worcestershire sauce

COMBINE all ingredients and heat thoroughly.

POUR over cooked fish.

Makes 1/2 cup.

SAUCES

WITH

TOMATOES

When cooking with tomatoes,

whether making sauces or gazpacho,

(see page 175),

add a piece of carrot.

It will cut the acidic taste,

making a sweeter product.

Great for fish, especially salmon or steelhead!

TOMATO HERB SAUCE

8 oz can tomato sauce	1 tsp lemon juice
1/4 cup water or white wine	1/2 tsp dried basil*
(sauterne or chablis)	1/2 tsp dried thyme
2 tbl oil or butter	

COMBINE all ingredients in a saucepan.

BRING sauce to a boil and simmer for five minutes.

(Great poured over fish in a shallow baking pan.
BAKE in 350° oven for thirty minutes.)

6 servings

*1 tablespoon fresh basil = 1 tsp dried.

Good over spaghetti or rice or ...

ITALIAN SAUCE

3 tbl oil   1 (1 lb.) can whole
1 onion, chopped   tomatoes
1 clove garlic, minced   1/4 tsp oregano
1 green pepper chopped   1 tsp salt
1 cup sliced mushrooms   1/2 cup red table wine
3 tbl rice flour   spaghetti or rice

HEAT the oil in a skillet and saute the onion, garlic,
    pepper, and mushrooms.

STIR in the flour.

ADD tomatoes, oregano and salt and stir until
    thickened. (This goes very well added to
    about a pound of meat.)

ADD the wine, and serve over your corn spaghetti
    or rice or biscuits.

4-6 servings

CHILI SAUCE MIX

3 tbl rice flour
1/2 cup instant minced onion
2 tbl chili powder
1 tbl salt

1/2 tsp red cayenne
     pepper
2 tsp instant minced
     garlic
2 tsp sugar
2 tsp ground cumin

COMBINE all ingredients and mix well.

ADJUST seasonings to taste by varying pepper and
     chili powder.

STORE in a labeled glass jar.

WINTER NIGHT CHILI

1 lb lean ground beef
2 (16 oz) cans of kidney
          beans

2 (16 oz) cans of
     tomatoes
1/4 cup chili sauce mix

BROWN the beef in a large skillet and drain.

ADD the rest of the ingredients.

SIMMER for 15 minutes, stirring occasionally.

4-6 servings

If you can tolerate yogurt...

PAN GRAVY

Instead of milk and flour,

ADD a little

yogurt and arrowroot powder

to your pan drippings

for a great, less fattening,

gravy!

This recipe makes it easy to have a safe salad dressing handy. It's a mix.

FRENCH DRESSING

1 cup sugar   2 tbl salt
2 tbl paprika   1/2 tsp onion powder
4 tsp dry mustard

COMBINE all ingredients and mix well.

STORE in a labeled glass jar.

TO MIX UP A BATCH...

5 tablespoons of the mix
3/4 cup olive or canola oil
1/4 cup cider or wine vinegar

COMBINE in a jar and SHAKE before use.

REFRIGERATE.

SALAD DRESSINGS - LESS FAT, MORE FLAVOR

SUBSTITUTE a darker, more flavorful oil, such as sesame oil for the oil in your recipe and cut the amount by as much as half.

SUBSTITUTE a more flavorful vinegar such as one of the rice vinegars or a fruity vinegar and cut down on your oil or use just the vinegar.

MAKE your own vinegars by steeping an herb in good white wine or cider vinegar for more flavor and use just the vinegar for your salad.

Just a reminder - if you need to avoid all grains, do not use white distilled vinegar as it is made from grains.

SIMPLE, SWEET SALAD DRESSING

1⁄3 cup wine vinegar   2⁄3 cup canola oil
1 tsp onion powder   2 tbl water
1 tsp honey   1 tbl crumbled bacon

MIX ingredients in a jar and shake.

EXCELLENT with fruit salads. (I like it with grape-
     fruit.)

REFRIGERATE.

*If you have to avoid mayonnaise, you will enjoy this
dressing for cole slaw, potato salad, or wheat-free
pasta salads.*

BOILED SALAD DRESSING

1 tsp dry mustard	1/3 cup wine or cider vinegar
1 tsp salt	1 egg yolk or egg replacer
1 tsp cornstarch or	1 tbl water
arrowroot*	
1 tbl sugar	

BLEND all ingredients until smooth.

POUR into a heavy saucepan or skillet.

COOK over medium heat until thickened, stirring
     constantly.

COOK 1 minute.

LET cool.

REFRIGERATE.

BASIC SALAD DRESSING

1 tsp salt	1/4 cup cider or wine
1/8 tsp black pepper	vinegar
1 tsp dry mustard	2/3 cup oil
	optional: 1 tsp Xanthan
	gum or to thicken

COMBINE all ingredients and mix well.

REFRIGERATE.

Different oils give a different taste, so be adventurous! Try adding anchovies, garlic, parsley, onions, etc.

Good for a salad dressing or a sandwich spread.

GUACAMOLE

1 large avocado	dash garlic salt
1/8 tsp salt	dash tobasco sauce

MASH avocado.

ADD remaining ingredients and mix well.

REFRIGERATE.

Something to "spread on the bread" is always a challenge.

SANDWICH SPREAD

6 onions	1 cup any wheat-free
6 tomatoes	flour
6 green peppers	1 pint prepared mustard
6 red peppers	1 pint vinegar
6 pickles	1 tsp turmeric
1/2 cup salt	1 quart of salad dress-
	ing

GRIND first 5 ingredients and put in salt.

LET stand 2 hours.

ADD sugar, flour, mustard, vinegar and turmeric.

BRING to a boil.

ADD salad dressing.

CAN in small jars.

SCREW lids on firmly.

SEAL by your normal procedure.

BLUEBERRY SAUCE

1 cup fresh or frozen blueberries 1 cup sugar
1/2 cup water   1 tbl lemon juice

SIMMER all the above for 10-15 minutes or until
    slightly thickened.

REMOVE from the heat.

Optional: add 1 tablespoon butter.

STIR and cool slightly.

You may add another cup of blueberries and serve.
Good over ice cream or French toast.

This is so good with turkey, chicken and pork.

PLUM SAUCE

1 can (1 lb.) whole purple plums	1/4 cup tomato chili sauce
2 tbl butter or margarine	2 tbl tamari (wheat-free soy sauce)
1 medium onion, chopped	
1/4 cup packed brown sugar	1 tsp ground ginger
	2 tsp lemon juice

DRAIN plums, remove pits.

PUREE plums and 2 tbl of the syrup and set aside.

PLACE butter in 1 quart microwavable dish.

MICROWAVE on HIGH for 20 seconds covered with waxed paper or loose plastic wrap.

ADD onion and MICROWAVE for 2 minutes on HIGH.

STIR in the rest of the ingredients.

MICROWAVE on HIGH for 3 minutes or until sauce thickens slightly.

PASS sauce at the table to spoon over individual servings.

KEEPS well in refrigerator.

SWEETS

There are in the end,
three things that last:
faith
hope,
and love,
and the greatest of
these is love.

1 Corinthians 13/13

Friend Steve Sinner says these were good, the day he installed our heating system, but were better served cold the day after!

PEACH DUMPLINGS

1 tbl butter or margarine	1/2 cup rice flour
1 cup sugar	1/2 cup bean flour
1 cup hot water	1 tsp Xanthan gum
2 cups sliced peaches	2 tsp baking powder
	1/2 tsp cinnamon
	dash salt
	3/4 cup cold water

COMBINE butter, sugar and hot water in a sauce pan.

BRING to a boil and cook until a syrup is formed.

ADD peaches and bring to a boil.

COMBINE dry ingredients and add the 3/4 cup cold water.

DROP the dumpling mixture by the spoonful into the boiling peach mixture.

COOK uncovered for 10 minutes.

COVER and simmer for 20 minutes. Serve while hot.

BLACKBERRY MUSH

4 cups blackberries   3/4 cup sugar
1/3 cup water   3 tbl cornstarch*
                                 1/2 tsp vanilla

ADD water to the washed berries and boil until
    berries are soft.

MASH and put through a strainer.

ADD sugar and cornstarch.

BOIL until thick, stirring constantly.

REMOVE from heat, add vanilla and chill.

*You may choose to use 3 tablespoons of tapioca.

You may substitute other berries or fruits.

CHEESE-FILLED PEARS

2 large or 4 small pears
1 cup (6 oz) Stilton or feta cheese
1/2 cup walnuts, chopped

WASH pears, cut in half and core.

CRUMBLE cheese and mix with chopped walnuts.

PILE into pear halves.

QUINCE APPLESAUCE

COOK one or two quinces

with each peck of apples

that you cook

for sauce.

(a peck is 1/4 of a bushel basket)

ADD honey to taste after cooking.

THE FLAVOR OF VANILLA

A vanilla pod makes a wonderful flavoring. Steeped in milk, for hot chocolate, it creates a marvelous drink, as does steeping it in wine. Steep the pod in boiling liquid for 10 to 15 minutes. When you have the flavor to your liking, rinse the pod in cold water and keep it in an air-tight container. It should keep for about 4 months. Keeping a piece of the pod in a container of sugar will flavor the sugar nicely and can be used to flavor a pudding or sauce.

THICKENERS

ARROWROOT FLOUR

Arrowroot is a thickener which can be used for soups, sauces, and puddings. It has no flavor of its own and is the easiest starch to digest. Arrowroot is best used at the end of your cooking just before boiling, as continued heating will cause it to lose its thickening ability. It is also good to use as a coating before frying as it makes a lighter and crispier coating than other flours. It can be found at your health food store.

CORNSTARCH

The advantage of cornstarch is that it thickens after reaching boiling point. It is very effective, but only if you are not allergic to corn!

FLOUR
Bring to a boil. Your mixture will thicken about 2-3 minutes after boiling. You affect flavor depending on what kind of flour you use.

TAPIOCA
Combine tapioca with fruit and liquids and allow to stand for 5 minutes. Bring to a boil and boil for 1 minute stirring constantly. Remove from heat and cool. Tapioca thickens as it cools.

In a recipe that you are converting and the recipe calls for:
        1 tablespoon of cornstarch, you may substitute
        1 tablespoon arrowroot or
        2 tablespoons tapioca or
        2 tablespoons flour

For a quick, creamy dessert...

VANILLA PUDDING

6 tbl arrowroot powder
4 cups soy or rice milk
1/2 cup maple syrup

pinch salt
2 tsp vanilla*
1/2 tsp nutmeg

DISSOLVE the arrowroot in 1/4 cup of the milk and set aside.

COMBINE the remaining milk, syrup and salt in a sauce pan.

BRING to a boil over medium heat, stirring constantly.

ADD the arrowroot mixture and stir until mixture thickens.

REMOVE from the heat.

STIR in vanilla and nutmeg.

POUR into serving dishes and refrigerate until serving time.

*You can store a piece of a vanilla bean in the mix, and remove before making the pudding.

CHOCOLATE PUDDING MIX

1 1/2 cup plus 2 tbl unsweetened 1 1/3 cup corn-
           cocoa powder   starch
3 1/4 cup granulated sugar   1/2 tsp salt

MIX well and store in a labeled container with a tight-
    fitting lid.

STORE in a cool, dry place.

NOW FOR SOME PUDDING!

2 3/4 cup soy or rice milk   2 tbl butter or margarine
2/3 cup pudding mix   1 tsp vanilla*

COMBINE mix and milk in medium saucepan.

COOK and stir over medium heat until mixture
    thickens.

COOK one minute longer.

REMOVE from heat and stir in butter or margarine
    and vanilla.

POUR pudding into 6 custard cups.

COVER each with plastic wrap.

REFRIGERATE for at least an hour.

6 servings

*You can store a piece of a vanilla bean in the mix, and remove before making the pudding.

Cathy Ehle, of Clackamas, Oregon, served on Grand Jury duty with me and gave me this recipe which comes from her mother, Marjorie Buchholz. I adapted it to be wheat and dairy-free.

CHOCOLATE PIE FILLING

1 1⁄2 cup sugar
1⁄4 tsp salt
2 tbl cornstarch
2 1⁄2 squares of baking
    chocolate

2 1⁄4 cups rice,soy or
    coconut milk
1 tbl rice flour
2 egg yolks*
1 tbl butter
1 tsp vanilla

COMBINE first 6 ingredients and bring to a boil.

BOIL for about 1 minute.

STIR in egg yolks and cook for 1 minute more.

ADD butter and vanilla.

POUR into baked pie crust (see pg 105) and refrigerate.

*Works well with egg substitute or no eggs at all!

*If you are in the mood for some quick safe ice cream,
you might want to try this...*

FROZEN DELIGHTS

PREPARE either pudding recipe. (pgs 207, 208)

COOL completely.

SPOON pudding into popsicle-type molds.

FREEZE overnight.

This recipe can be applied to many fruits and flavorings.

APPLE TAPIOCA

1/2 cup minute tapioca	2 tsp lemon juice
1/2 tsp salt	3 cups water
1/2 to 1 cup brown or white sugar	4 cups sliced apples
	Cinnamon, cloves, allspice

COMBINE tapioca, salt, sugar, lemon juice.

MIX with the water.

BRING to a boil over medium heat, stirring constantly.

POUR over fruit in a 9"X14" greased baking dish.

SPRINKLE spices on top of apples.

COVER and bake at 325° for about 45 minutes.

Serves 6

CRAN-RASPBERRY SORBET

1/4 cup water
1/4 cup sugar
3 1/4 cups cranberry-raspberry juice, chilled

SIMMER water and sugar in saucepan over low heat
  until sugar is dissolved.

COOL to room temperature.

ADD cranberry-raspberry juice.

FREEZE in the bowl of an ice cream machine
  according to the maker's instructions.

Makes 5 cups or 10 servings

Librarian, Valerie McQuaid, used to make this for her daughter, Kerry. You can play with this recipe by adding fruit or fruit syrups.

ALMOST ICE CREAM

4 eggs   1/2 cup honey
2 cups rice or soy milk   1/2 cup corn oil
1 tsp vanilla

BEAT all ingredients together.

FREEZE in a quart container.

You can also flavor the ice cream by letting a piece of vanilla bean soak in the milk overnight. Remove the bean and save for another day.

One of Dr. John Green's favorites...

MAPLE TOPPING

Add a little oil or butter

to 2 cups maple syrup.

Cook to soft ball stage

or harder for popcorn balls.

"Yummy"!!

Great over "Rice Dream"

or gingerbread.

BLUEBERRY RHUBARB CONSERVE

3 cups rhubarb in 1 inch
    pieces
3 cups fresh or dry
    frozen blueberries
5 cups sugar

2 small packages rasp-
    berry gelatin
juice of 1⁄2 lemon

MIX rhubarb, blueberries, sugar and lemon juice and
    let stand overnight in refrigerator.

BRING mixture to a boil over low heat & cook for 12
    minutes.

REMOVE from heat and stir in gelatin.

POUR into hot jars and seal with paraffin.

I can hear my mother, Rose, saying "Waste not, want not!" The Honnold family never did!

APPLE JELLY

peelings from 6-7 apples
2 cups water
1 tbl powdered pectin (or 1 tbl vinegar.)
1 1/3 cups granulated sugar
pinch of salt
pinch of cream of tartar

BOIL peelings for 20 minutes in water.

STRAIN off juice and measure 1 1/2 cups into a pan
        adding a pinch of tartar.

LET simmer for 5 minutes.

ADD pectin (or vinegar)

ADD granulated sugar and a pinch of salt.

LET it fast boil for 7 minutes.

POUR into glasses and top with paraffin.

WHIPPED PARAFFIN

After you put a layer of paraffin on your jams or
jellies, you might want to put a decorative layer of
whipped paraffin on top.

MELT paraffin in a can large enough to hold the
blades of your mixer.

WHIP paraffin just before it begins to set as it cools.

BEAT until it becomes a fluffy foam.

PUT a small piece of aluminum foil over the first layer
of paraffin on your jar.

USE a knife to apply and decorate the top of your
jar.

(Never throw down the sink as it clogs the drain!)

VERY LIKE APPLETS

2 tbl plain gelatin   1 cup walnuts or almonds
1 1/4 cup applesauce   1 tsp vanilla
2 cups raw or brown sugar

DISSOLVE gelatin in 1/2 cup of warm applesauce
     and set aside.

COMBINE remaining applesauce with sugar.

BOIL for 10 minutes.

ADD gelatin mixture and boil for 15 minutes stirring
     constantly.

REMOVE from heat and ADD vanilla and nuts.

POUR into greased 8 X 8" pan.

LET stand overnight.

CUT into squares and dust with powdered sugar.

Yum-m-m-m.

Use a thick apricot or grape puree for two other tasty
variations.

In addition to his wonderful wood creations, Craftsman extraordinaire, Jim Knull, makes these old fashioned...

HOREHOUND DROPS

6 tbl horehound leaves and stems
1 1/2 cups hot water
3 1/2 cups brown sugar

CRUSH the herbs and place in a teapot.

COVER with boiling water and steep for 30 minutes.

STRAIN and POUR this liquid over the brown sugar.

MIX in a saucepan .

BRING to a boil.

BOIL until the mixture reaches the hard crack stage.
     (300°)

POUR into a buttered pan and cut into squares.

Also, very good for coughs and sore throats!

Enid France of Alexandria, Virginia shares this sinful recipe with us.

NUTTY CHOCOLATE TRUFFLES

1/4 cup light cream*   1/4 cup butter, softened
6 oz semisweet baking   1/2 cup coarsely chopped
    chocolate   toasted walnuts
                             confectioners' sugar

Optional: 2 tbl orange or raspberry-flavored liqueur
             or dark rum.
             (make sure the liqueur is grain-free)

BRING cream to boiling in small saucepan.

BOIL for 2 minutes, or until reduced by half.

REMOVE from heat.

BREAK up chocolate and add.

STIR until chocolate melts.

ADD liqueur if desired.

STIR in butter and nuts and mix well.

SPOON mixture into soup-size bowl.

REFRIGERATE until firm, about 1 hour.

FILL a custard cup about halfway with sugar.

SCOOP chilled chocolate with teaspoon and roll between palms of hands to shape into 1 inch balls. (This will be messy!)

DROP the chocolate ball into the sugar; toss to coat it.

PLACE truffles in individual candy cups and store in a covered container in the refrigerator until ready to serve.

BRING truffles to room temperature 15 minutes before serving.

*I have used rice milk and non-dairy margarine with success. Avoid powdered sugar if you have to avoid corn, as it contains cornstarch!

MISCELLANEOUS

HOW TO BE
REALLY ALIVE!

Live juicy. Stamp out conformity. Stay in bed all day. Dream of gypsy wagons. Find snails making love. Develop an astounding appetite for books. Drink sunsets. Draw out your feelings. Amaze yourself. Be ridiculous. Stop worrying. Now. If not now, then when? Make yes your favorite word. Marry yourself. Dry your clothes in the sun. Eat mangoes naked. Keep toys in the bathtub. Spin yourself dizzy. Hang upside down. Follow a child. Celebrate an old person. Send a love letter to your self. Be advanced. Try endearing. Invent new ways to love. Transform negatives. Delight someone. Wear pajamas to a drive in movie. Allow yourself to feel rich without money. Be who you truly are and the money will follow. Believe in everything. You are always on your way to a miracle.

THE MIRACLE IS YOU

*Found on a San Francisco bulletin board, this reminder to come alive comes from **Heather Van Rykn** of Nuveen & Co.*

"Gorp" has been a traditional trail mix or snack for our family's outings.

GORP

1 cup raisins   1/2 cup almonds or
                                           cashews
1 cup soy nuts or peanuts 1/2 cup M & M's or
1/2 cup coconut   chocolate chips

STORE in an air-tight container.

Ginger is soothing to the digestive tract.

GINGER TEA

Ginger root   Three cups of good well
1 tsp anise or fennel seeds   water

SIMMER 10 thin slices of ginger root in the water for
        15 minutes.

ADD anise or fennel seeds with the ginger to make
      the tea naturally sweet.

STRAIN and enjoy.

*Never any risk of corn syrup or preservatives when
you make your own!!*

GRAPE JUICE

2 cups grapes per 1 quart jar   1 cup sugar per jar

FILL each jar with grapes and sugar.

ADD water allowing 1/2 inch head space when fill-
      ing jars.

SCREW lids on tightly.

PUT jars in canner and cover with water.

BRING to a boil.

BOIL for 10 minutes.

TURN off and let stand until cold.

You may dilute with cold water if desired.

BRANDIED CIDER

1 quart cider	4 whole cloves
3 tbl honey	1 whole nutmeg
2 tbl lemon juice	1 2" piece cinnamon
	1/4 - 1/3 cup brandy

COMBINE cider, honey and lemon.

PLACE spices in double thickness cheesecloth and
      tie.

ADD cheesecloth bag to cider mixture.

COVER and heat but don't boil.

STIR in brandy and serve.   6 servings

Many Scandinavian countries have something similar to this little German holiday beverage!

GLUHWEIN

1 bottle of Claret	1 inch piece of cinna-
6 lumps/teaspoons sugar	mon
3 whole cloves	3 strips of orange peel
	3 strips lemon peel

HEAT all ingredients in a saucepan, but don't boil.

STRAIN into a pitcher.

THRUST in a hot poker - if you want to be traditional - and serve!

KAHLUA

2 oz instant coffee*	1 vanilla bean cut into 4
2 cups boiling water	pieces
3 1/2 cups sugar	1 quart (4 cups) brandy
	1 pint (2 cups) vodka

ADD coffee to water slowly, mixing well.

COOL.

PLACE vanilla bean pieces in a 2 1⁄2 quart jar.

ADD cooled coffee mixture.

COMBINE the coffee mixture, brandy and vodka.

COVER tightly and let stand for 30 days.

REMOVE the vanilla bean pieces and store Kahlua
    in small bottles.

2 1⁄2 quarts

Vodka should be distilled from grapes or potatoes
not grains.

*Yes, Emily, it has to be **instant** coffee. Regular just
won't do it! (Emily is my friend and editor!)

HOMEMADE APPLE PECTIN

The reason you are advised not to use overripe fruit
when making jams and jellies is because it has little
pectin and thus is responsible for a good deal of
runny jams and jellies. Thus, choose apples which
are at their best when you are making pectin. Slightly
underripe fruit has the highest pectin content. Also
pectin is concentrated in the skins and core of the
fruit so do not peel or core the fruit.

8 medium tart apples
4 cups water
2 tbl lemon juice

WASH apples and cut into small pieces without peel-
ing.

REMOVE stems and blossom ends.

PUT apples in a large pot and barely cover with
water.

COVER and cook slowly for about 40 minutes or
until fruit is quite soft.

POUR cooked fruit into a dampened jelly bag.

LET hang overnight to extract as much juice as possible without squeezing.

BOIL this juice rapidly for 15 minutes.

POUR boiling juice into sterilized jars and seal.

PROCESS 5 minutes in a boiling water bath or keep
refrigerated.

You can use this same process with red currants,
just mash them before letting them drip.

To use this recipe as a replacement for Xanthan gum
you will need to boil the liquid down to perhaps 1/4

of its volume and include it in the total liquid that you add to your recipe. For example: If your recipe calls for 1 cup of water, you will pour the pectin into the measuring cup and fill with water to the 1 cup level. Because everyone will boil the pectin to a slightly different level, you will have to experiment with how much works to hold your baked product together.

HERBAL NOTES

A "Bouquet Garni" is a way of flavoring a

soup or stew without

having to fish out the sprigs of herbs.

Try a few sprigs of...

thyme, a bay leaf and 2-3 fresh parsley sprigs.

or

a stalk of celery, sprig of lovage,

marjoram or savory, and an orange peel.

Tie in a bundle so they can be removed at the

end of the cooking time.

ROASTING NUTS

Hazelnuts or filberts

> SPREAD shelled nuts in shallow pan.
>
> ROAST in 275° oven for 20-30 minutes.
>
> REMOVE skins by wrapping in a dish towel and let nuts steam for 1 minute.
>
> RUB the nuts in the towel to remove skins.
>
> STORE in refrigerator or freezer.

Walnuts

> SPREAD shelled halves or pieces in shallow pan.
>
> ROAST in 350° oven for 15 minutes.
>
> STORE in refrigerator or freezer.

Almonds

> SPREAD shelled nuts in shallow pan.
>
> ROAST at 325° for about 15-20 minutes.
>
> STIR often.

Note: You preserve the nutrients by always roasting **before** chopping.

CANNING

DRIED FRUITS & NUTS

STERILIZE jars at 150° in the <u>oven</u> for 20 minutes.

FILL sterilized jars with dried fruits, nuts, grains, or pasta and put on lids.

PLACE in oven for 30-40 minutes at 150-175°.

TAKE out of oven and allow to cool.

FRUITS WITHOUT SUGAR

STERILIZE jars.

POUR in 1-2 cups boiling water.

ADD 1 large spoonful honey.

DROP in 1 1/2 cup fruit.

ADD boiling water to top and seal.

Powdered sugar has cornstarch in it...
Just in case you cannot tolerate corn,
here is a substitute to help you with
your candy recipes.

SUPERFINE SUGAR

You can make

superfine sugar by

processing granulated sugar

in a blender for

one minute!

A completely natural potpourri can be more tolerable to those of us with sensitive noses!

POTPOURRI

peel of 1 grapefruit   4 cups water
peel of 2 oranges   2 cinnamon sticks
peel of 2 lemons   1 tbl cloves
                             1 tbl allspice

BRING to a boil.

SIMMER to provide fragrance throughout your
      house.

REFRIGERATE between simmerings!

USE a potato peeler to obtain the "zest" or citrus
      peel and you will not lose the oil in the skin.
      Collect and save your peels in a well-sealed
      bag in the freezer.

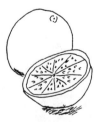

Chances are, if you are sensitive to foods, that you are also sensitive to chemicals in your environment. Calendula is a lovely flower that has proved to be kind to the skin and when added to an olive oil and beeswax base, makes a more than satisfactory skin moisturizer. You will feel the difference. But only make a little at first just to be sure you are not sensitive to these ingredients.

CALENDULA CREAM

CHOP 3 or 4 Calendula flowers.

PUT in a clear glass jar.

COVER with 1 cup of olive oil and put the lid on.

PLACE in the sun and let sit for at least 2 weeks.*

STERILIZE small glass jars and lids by boiling for 3
      minutes.

      When you are ready to mix up a batch...

STRAIN through clean cotten cloth.

HEAT oil in a small glass or jar in a double boiler or
      in a electric skillet with 1 inch of water.

*Editor, Emily says, "This may be tricky in Oregon!"
(to find 2 weeks of sun!)

ADD 1/2 ounce or more of beeswax in small pieces.
1/2 ounce makes a cream that is easily
spreadable. The amount used determines
heaviness

STIR until dissolved.

POUR hot mixture carefully into your jars.

LABEL and keep in the refrigerator
Yes, labelling is important even if you think
you have a good memory. Someone might
accidentally moisturize the inside of their
stomach!

A jar of your cream will keep outside of the refrigerator if you are careful to use an applicator and not
your fingers. (Your fingers are more likely to intro-
duce mold.)

*Good as a night cream or for chapped hands. Bo-
rax is a skin softener. Zinc heals irritated skin.*

ALMOND CREAM

3 fl. oz almond oil	1/2 tsp Borax dissolved
1 oz beeswax	in 2 fl. oz water
1 tsp anhydrous lanolin	1 tsp zinc oxide
	2 fl. oz almond oil

Use a double boiler or a small pyrex container set in a skillet of water. This is called a water bath.

BREAK up the beeswax into little pieces, the easier for it to melt.

HEAT the beeswax and lanolin in a water bath until the beeswax is melted.

DO not let the wax simmer.

REMOVE from the heat and add the 3 fluid oz of almond oil slowly.

In a separate dish, MIX the zinc oxide and 2 fluid oz of almond oil to make it smooth.

ADD the zinc mixture to the beeswax beating continuously.

DISSOLVE the borax in 2 oz of bottled water or water that has been boiled.

ADD the borax mixture and beat until cool.

You may add a drop of scented oil if you like.

See page 241 for storing instructions.

A word of CAUTION: Don't be heating wax with small children around, nor do you want to get distracted and leave it. You need to watch it carefully.

When decorating with

FRESH FLOWERS,

help flowers to last longer

with this recipe:

1 qt water

1 tbl sugar

2 tbl lime or lemon juice

1/2 tsp liquid bleach

If you are sensitive to foods, chances are you are sensitive to some of the chemicals around you. Cutting down on the chemicals is like unloading the dump truck before it can dump. Here are some ways to simplify your cleaning.

NATURAL CLEANERS

BE SURE TO LABEL ALL CLEANERS CLEARLY.

wooden floors   1 cup vinegar in a pail of water.

mold & mildew   3/4 cup bleach to 1 gallon
                                  water
                       You can buy paint with mold
                       and mildew killer in it.

mildew preventive   use full-strength vinegar to
                           clean fridge. Borax in water
                           works, also. Sprinkle borax
                           in mold-prone areas like the
                           bottom of the garbage can.

perspiration stains   sponge with white vinegar.
                             Work on wrong side with right
                             side on an old towel.

blood   blot with cold water then
               dampen with diluted hydrogen
               peroxide rinse.

chocolate   sponge with warm, soapy
                          water.

coffee, tea	sponge with warm water or use glycerine.
ballpoint ink	treat with cold water, then gently rub with diluted rubbing alcohol or spray with hair spray and blot with a soft cloth.
grease and oil	dampen then lightly apply hand dishwashing detergent; rinse. If this does not work, dry clean.
drain cleaner	pour 1/2 cup baking soda down drain. Follow with 1/2 cup vinegar. Cover drain and wait 5 minutes. Uncover drain and pour a kettle of boiling water down the drain. Repeat if necessary.
window cleaner	mix equal parts ammonia, iso-propyl alcohol & water and pour into spray bottle. Spray on glass or mirrors and wipe clean.
all-purpose cleaner	mix 1 quart wam water, 1 tsp liquid soap, 1 tsp borax and a squeeze of lemon or table spoon of vinegar.
preventive oven cleaner	sprinkle salt on a spill right away. Brush away when cool.

tea-kettle lime deposits	boil water and vinegar: let stand overnight.
rusted pliers	soak overnight in vinegar!
brass or copper cleaner	vinegar or lemon and salt

MAKE A COMMITMENT TO A HEALTHY HOME ENVIRONMENT

1. Do install an exhaust fan that vents outside over your gas stove to remove the nitrogen-dioxide fumes.

2. Have your cat tested by a vet for toxoplasmosis, and if it's found to be a carrier, have it treated to eliminate the parasite. Don't eat any raw or undercooked meat or feed any to your cat. Change the litter box daily before the eggs become infective. Wear gloves when you do. Wear gloves when gardening. Wash all vegetables well. And wash your hands often—especially after handling the cat or raw foods.

3. Do transfer boxed or bagged grain products, including flour, rice, pasta and cereals, to glass, metal or plastic airtight containers. And keep them in a dry, cool place off the floor to prevent insect infestation and mold.

4. Make your environment reflect you and your changes. Planning for beauty, comfort, humor and solace make coming home a joy.

5. Drain the rain. Make seasonal checks to free your gutters and spouts of leaves and debris to prevent interior leaks, and dampness which are "open house" to termites.

6. Mix borax with your wallpaper paste to ward off mildew and insects.

7. Discourage ants by sealing off cracks where they're entering with putty or petroleum jelly. Try sprinkling red pepper on floors and countertops.

8. Don't mix chlorine bleach with either ammonia, a toilet bowl cleaner or any other household chemical. It produces a deadly gas.

9. If you live with a smoker, consider one of the round-the-clock air-cleaner devices. Negative-ion generators were found most effective as smoke cleaners.

10. Vacuum and wash pet areas regularly with a mixture made by placing a thinly sliced lemon in a pint of boiling water and steeping overnight. Strain and sponge on pet. Apply daily if necessary.

11. Make a neat, cozy bed for your dog in winter by filling a burlap bag with hay or straw and placing it in his doghouse.

12. Banish roaches by sprinkling boric acid (or using a squeeze bottle) into moldings and crevices. This kills them slowly. It may take 6 days or longer, but they will not develop a

resistance to it. Boric acid is not absorbed by
your skin or if inhaled, but is poisonous if eaten,
so take necessary precautions for children and
pets.

13. Be wary of using earthenware pottery or pre-
1930 pewter and some modern imports which
can have lead in them which can leach into
acidic foods. Get an expert's opinion of its
safety.

14. Choose photoelectric model smoke detectors.
The ionization types contain radioactive material that is almost certain to be released if the
unit is damaged in a serious fire, presenting a
real hazard to you and the firefighters. Get
recycling information for disposing of these
detectors properly.

15. Break in a new toothbrush every three months
or so. Worn bristles are not as effective.

16. Sunlight and air circulation discourage musty
mildew-prone rooms like the bath and basement, as well as provide us with year round
physical and psychological benefits from the
natural beauty of light.

17. Don't expose aerosol containers to flame or
sun or boiling water. Pump dispensers are
safer.

18. Chlorine bleach chemically alters the elastic in the waistbands of your underwear and can cause a nasty skin irritation.

19. Lead in the inks of color news print or magazines can be released into the room when burned in your fireplace.

20. Keep baking soda accessible in your kitchen to grab quickly to squelch a pan fire.

21. Soak produce you haven't grown yourself in a basin filled with water and 1/4 cup of vinegar before scrubbing with a vegetable brush under running water.

22. Keep firewood 30 feet away from your house. And clear out your basement and crawl space of unwanted wood to help discourage termite infestation. The trouble with termites is that once you spot them, there's nothing short of chlordane—a potent and potentially cancer-causing substance—that will knock 'em dead.

23. Many whiteners and fabric softeners can cause skin irritation. Try an additional water rinse or another product.

24. Keep leaves, weeds and grass under control and away from the perimeter of your home to eliminate mold spores that can make you wheeze.

25. Save major paint, papering, reflooring projects for warmer weather so you can open windows for extended periods to ventilate.

26. Wash humidifiers weekly and drip pans from your frost-free refrigerator monthly with a stiff brush and hydrogen peroxide to kill moisture-loving bacteria and fungi that can cause respiratory problems.

27. Aerosol "deodorizers" temporarily mask odors by numbing your sense of smell. Prevent odors by opening a box of baking soda.

28. Do a daily airing of your home. "Use with adequate ventilation" means use a fan or vent with an open window. Consider an air-to-air heat exchanger for fresh air without substantial heat loss.

29. Mold can penetrate deeper into food than is obvious. Trimming off mold is not always enough. Throw it away.

30. Open your garage door before starting your car and allow the carbon monoxide time to dissipate before closing up for the evening.

31. Air out washing machine awhile, so it's fresh next time.

32. Blankets and pillows become dust-free after a 5 minute stay in your dryer on "fluff". (no heat!)

33. "Plant an herb garden. A tiny space can grow lots of tasty perennial herbs. Also, add a few vegetables. Gardening increases your lifespan"...Dr. John Green M.D.

34. "Buy organically grown foods. They're much higher in nutrients and less apt to contain pesticide residues,"...Dr. John Green M.D.

Much of this excellent information comes from a large list of dos and don'ts for a healthy home environment that has been in my files for a long while. I do not remember where it came from and therefore apologize for not giving credit.

INDEX

All barley muffins 47
Allergies, about xxiv
Almond butter cookies 138
Almond cakes 130
Almond cream 238
Almonds 233
Almost ice cream 213
Amish pie 108
Amish friendship bread 30
Amish shoo-fly pie 109
Anise cookies 131
Antipasto 168
Apple cobbler 110
Apple kugel 166
Apple jelly 216
Apple oatmeal muffins 50
Apple pectin 229
Apple roll 101
Apple tapioca 211
Applesauce, quince 204
Applesauce raisin cake 78
Applets, very like 218
Apricot glaze 96
Arrowroot 206
Bagels 35
Baking powder xix
Baking soda xix
Barley Bread 21
    Muffin 47
Basic salad dressing 194
Basic Dijon-style mustard 181
Bean flour xii
Biscuit Mix 60
Biscuit mix two - without shortening 63
Biscuits 61
    Cheese biscuits 62
Biscuits two 64
Blackberry mush 202
Blueberry rhubarb conserve 215
Blueberry pie 113

Blueberry sauce   196
Boiled oatmeal cookies 133
Bouquet garni   232
Bran loaf   43
Brandied cider   227
Bread flour mix   15
Bread machines   3, 7
Bread making, manual   10
Bread, seasoning the   19
Bread, stewed   166
Breads, non-yeast
    Bran loaf   43
    Brown   39
    Brown, grain-free   41
    Italian biscuit   45
    Strawberry   44
Breads, yeast
    Amish friendship   30
    Barley   21
    High five rye   25
    Kamut   16
    Sourdough   32, 33, 34
    Spelt   13, 14
    Sweet wheatless   23
    Walrus   17, 18
Brown bread   39
Brown bread grain-free 41
Buns, sweet raised   66
Butterscotch ice box cookies   129
Cabbage,
    Country   158
    Red   159
Cabbages and kings...and apple pies   112
Cakes
    Applesauce raisin   78
    Cherry Clafoutis   87
    Cider   80
    Country French   97
    Dairy torte   85
    Dickens of an English plum pudding   94
    Fudge torte   83
    Granma's plum pudding   92

Jam	76	
Non-dairy torte	87	
P C chocolate cake	100	
Passover sponge	77	
Prune flan	81	
Sand	75	
Steamed whiskey pudding		90
Strawberry tofu torte	82	
Topsey turvey pudding	89	
Calendula cream	237	
Candy		
Horehound drops	219	
Nutty chocolate truffles	220	
Very like applets	218	
Canning	234	
Dried fruits and nuts	234	
Fruits without sugar		
Carrot bran muffins	51	
Catsup, just	179	
Cheese biscuits	62	
Cheese-filled pears	203	
Cheese-stuffed squash	161	
Cherry Clafoutis	87	
Chickpea flour	xii	
Chili sauce mix	189	
Chili, winter night	189	
Chocolate cream pie	121	
Chocolate glaze	85	
Chocolate pie filling	209	
Cider, brandied	227	
Cider cake	80	
Cider soup	173	
Cinnamon raisin muffins	49	
Cleaners, natural	241	
Clucking pear stir-fry	160	
Cobbler, peach	111	
Coconut cookies	134	
Cones, ice cream	146	
Conserve, blueberry rhubarb	215	
Cookies		
Almond butter	138	
Almond cakes	130	

Anise	131	
Boiled oatmeal	133	
Butterscotch ice box	129	
Coconut	134	
Gingersnaps	139	
Heifer tongues	140	
Lebkuchen	141	
Leckerle	143	
Oat	132	
Peanut butter	137	
Springerle	144	
Supermouse bars	136	
Tofu bars	135	
Cornstarch	206	
Country cabbage	158	
Country French cake	97	
Crackers, sunflower	72	
Cran-raspberry sorbet	212	
Creams,		
Almond	238	
Calendula	237	
Creme fraiche	89	
Dairy torte	85	
Dickens of an English plum pudding		94
Drinks,		
Brandied cider	227	
Ginger tea	226	
Gluhwein	228	
Grape juice	226	
Kahlua	228	
Dumplings, peach	201	
Egg replacer	xx	
Eggfree Mayonnaise	184	
Elderberry pie	119	
Environment, healthy home	244	
Equipment	xiv	
Filbert rice	163	
Filberts	233	
Filling, orange custard	99	
Flour substitutions	xxvi	
Flours	xv	
Flowers, fresh	240	

French dressing 191
Fried green tomatoes 164
Fried green tomatoes for another day 165
Frozen delights 210
Fruits without sugar 234
Fudge torte 83
Garbanzo bean flour xii
Garden potato soup 174
Gazpacho soup 175
Gingersnaps 139
Ginger tea 226
Glaze,
      Chocolate 85
      Apricot 96
      Lebkuchen 142
Gluhwein 228
Gluten xi, xiv
Gorp 225
Granma's plum pudding 92
Grape juice 226
Gravy, pan 190
Green tomato pie 115
Guacamole 194
Hard sauce 95
Hazelnuts 233
Heifer tongues 140
Hearty stuffed potatoes 154
Herbal notes 232
High five rye bread 25
Holiday sweet potatoes 155
Home environment 244
Homemade mincemeat pie 123
Hops tea 12
Horehound drops 219
Ice cream,
      almost 213
      cran-raspberry sorbet 212
      frozen delights 210
Ice cream cones 146
Italian biscuit bread 45
Italian sauce 188
Jam cake 76

Jelly, apple 216
Juice, grape 226
Kahlua 228
Kale soup 171
Kamut bread 16
Ketchup (see catsup) 179
Kugel, apple 166
Lasagne, potato 156
Lebkuchen 141
Lebkuchen glaze 142
Leckerle 143
Lefse, Norwegian 68
Manual bread making 10
Maple topping 214
Mayonnaise, eggfree 184
Measuring tips xxiii
Milk substitutes xxi
Mincement, homemade 123
MJ's orange muffins 52
Moby Dick chowder 172
Muffins
    All barley 47
    Apple oatmeal 50
    Carrot bran 51
    Cinnamon raisin 49
    MJ's Orange 52
    Oat bran 55, 56
    Poppy seed 54
    Teff 48
Muffin mix 53
Mush, blackberry 202
Mustard,
    Basic Dijon-style 181
    Spicy 180
Natural cleaners 241
Non-dairy torte 87
Noodles 69
    Rice 70
Norwegian lefse 68
Nuts, roasting 233
Nutty chocolate truffles 220
Oat bran muffins 55, 56

Oat cookies   132, 133
Orange custard filling   99
Pancakes,   59
    Mix, pancake   58
    Pancakes two   64
    Sourdough   31
Pan gravy   190
Paraffin, whipped   217
Passover sponge cake 77
P C chocolate cake   100
Peach cobbler   111
Peach crunch   117
Peach dumplings   201
Peanut butter cookies   137
Pears, cheese-filled   203
Pecan butter sauce   185
Pectin, homemade apple   229
Pesto   182
Pie crust   105, 106
Pie filling, chocolate   209
Pies
    Amish shoo-fly   109
    Amish   108
    Apple cobbler   110
    Blueberry   113
    Cabbages and kings...and apple pies   112
    Chocolate cream   121
    Elderberry   119
    Green tomato   115
    Mincemeat   123
    Peach cobbler   111
    Peach crunch   117
    Plum   118
    Raisin pecan   122
    Rhubarb raspberry custard   114
    Strawberry   107
    Sugar-free strawberry   125
Pizza crust   152
Plum pudding,
    Dickens of an English   94
    Granma's   92
Plum sauce   197

Plum pie	118	
Poppy seed muffins	54	
Potato lasagne	156	
Potato soup, garden	174	
Potatoes, Hardy stuffed	154	
Holiday sweet	155	
Potpourri	236	
Pretzels, rye	70	
Prune flan	81	
Pudding,		
Apple tapioca		211
Chocolate		208
Granma's plum		92
Steamed whiskey		90
Topsey, turvey		89
Vanilla		207
Pudding mix, chocolate	208	
Quince applesauce	204	
Raised sweet buns	66	
Raisin pecan pie	122	
Red cabbage	159	
Rhubarb raspberry custard	114	
Rice flour	xii	
Rice,		
Filbert		163
Stir fried		162
Ring around the vegies	151	
Roasting nuts	233	
Rye pretzels	70	
Salad dressing,		
Basic		194
Boiled		193
French		191
Guacamole		194
Less fat, more flavor		192
Simple, sweet		192
Salt	xv	
Sand cake	75	
Sandwich spread	195	
Sauces		
Blueberry		196
Chili sauce mix		189
Creme fraiche		89

Hard 95
Italian 188
Just catsup 179
Pan gravy 190
Pecan butter 185
Pesto 182
Plum 197
Tomato herb 187
With tomatoes 186
Seasoning the bread 19
Shortcake two 65
Shortening xv
Sorbet, cran-raspberry 212
Soups
Cider 173
Garden potato 174
Gazpacho 175
Kale 171
Moby Dick chowder 172
Sourdough 27
Bread 30, 32, 33, 34
Pancakes 31
Starter 27
Spelt bread 13, 14
Spicy mustard 180
Springerle cookies 144
Squash, cheese-stuffed 161
Steamed whiskey pudding 90
Stewed bread 166
Stir fried rice 162
Stir-fry, clucking pear 160
Strawberry pie 107, 125
Strawberry bread 44
Strawberry tofu torte 82
Sugar xviii
Sugar-free strawberry pie 125
Sunflower crackers 72
Superfine sugar 235
Supermouse bars 136
Sweet dough 120
Sweet potatoes, holiday 155
Sweet wheatless bread 23

Syrup   102
Tapioca   206,
        Apple   211
Tea, ginger   226
Teff muffins   48
Thickeners   206
Tofu bars   135
Tomato herb sauce   187
Tomatoes,
        green fried   164
        green fried for another day   165
        green...pie   115
Toppings
        maple   214
        blueberry   196
Topsey turvey pudding   89
Tort, chocolate   83
Truffles, nutty chocolate   220
Vanilla pudding   207
Vanilla, the flavor of   205
Vegies, ring around the   151
Very like applets   218
Waffles   59, 65
Walnuts   233
Walrus bread   17, 18
Whiskey pudding, steamed   90
Whipped parraffin   217
Winter night chili   189
Xanthan gum   xvi
Yeast   xvii